Hey Man, We're the Band

(Where Do We Set Up?)

by

Rick "BigBassMan" Joyner

Front cover and Author photo by Meghann Acreman

Interior artwork by Matthew Joyner

Dedication

To Vicki, Matthew, Meghann, Melody, and Mac, you are my inspiration, my joy, and my life. You've had to sit through way too many of my gigs, and I thank you.

To my father, Walter; my mom, Genetta; my brother, Carl; and my sister, Sue, I wish you were here for this. I know you would be proud.

To my brother Randol, you were smart enough to get out of the music business before it was too late.

To Randy and Kenny, I miss you, my friends! You left us way too soon. I can't wait to jam with you again in Heaven.

To all the weekend warrior musicians, keep the faith, my brothers and sisters!

Contents

THE ROAD

CLOSING

Introduction

So You Want To Be a Musician?

Rock On!

So you bought yourself an electric guitar from an online store and an amplifier from a local pawnshop, and you've studied your Mel Bay instruction manuals until the pages are torn and tattered. Now you're ready for the big time, right? Maybe…or maybe not. Before you quit your day job, buy an old Greyhound bus, and paint "Bill Clore and the Clorettes" on the side, you really need to read this book from cover to cover, maybe more than once. Think of this as a manual, of sorts, your standard operating procedure created by folks who have gone before you. For the most part, this is a collection of humorous stories, mostly about the bad or weird things that can happen to a musician or band. I would love to tell you that everything will be different for you, that you will experience only the good and none of the bad and ugly, but every musician past and present knows that you must push on through the bad to get to the good. Hey, maybe that's why musicians love to play the blues! It would also be really nice if this book could help you steer clear of some of the pitfalls others have experienced, but you are a musician. What does this mean? Clearly, you probably won't listen to me anyway. I guess the most I can expect is that this will at least allow you to identify with other musicians when you experience these things yourself.

I don't want to piss anyone off, especially in the second paragraph, but I have to ask you a very tough question: Are you any good? I ask because it is very important that you set the right expectation for what you want to do with your music. Please hear me out here: Not everyone is as talented as the unforgettable Jimi Hendrix, but rest assured there is a place for those who aren't. The most important thing is that you aren't so blinded by the stars in your eyes that you become naïve to reality. Don't expect to be ready for a recording contract the minute you learn your first minor chord. I know that's a great moment for all of us, but there's a bit more to it than that. I'm reminded of the line at the end of *Bill and Ted's Bogus Journey*: "Dude, we still don't know how to play. Maybe we ought to get good, Ted."

Musicians fall into a wide array of categories, but you can generally place them into one of the four following groups. First, there are those with the talent, the drive, and the breaks that will allow them to do just about anything they want in the music business. Others have the talent and drive but never catch the breaks; these are your typical "local legends," and none of us can understand why they didn't make it. Furthermore, there are those folks who have the talent, but they either have no drive or tend to let other things get in the way of their music. Finally, there are the folks with no talent but lots of ambition. This last group usually sets themselves up for a lot of heartache. It's not my intention to judge anyone's ability or drive; I just think it's best if those with limited wherewithal do not to expect too much, because that may only lead to disappointment.

I have arranged this book with the musician in mind. In other words, each story is short enough to accommodate one trip to the restroom, there are no big words, and I've written it with a complete lack of sophistication—in a way even most drummers can understand. While non-musicians might appreciate the humor in these stories, real musicians will roar, because they have been there. Every story is absolutely factual, though I may have exercised a wee bit of literary license in just a few places. In some cases, I've combined a couple stories or experiences and assigned them to one person; as they say, some of the names and locations have been changed to protect the guilty and to keep me from getting sued. I may have even attached someone else's story to my own name to keep their dignity intact. The point is, I can almost guarantee that every story has happened to someone other than the person or persons I have written about. Just change the names and locations, and these stories might very well be yours. The great majority are recollections of my own experiences, and the remainder came from close friends. My research for this book couldn't have been easier: I only had to get a bunch of old musicians together, throw in a case of beer, and turn on the tape recorder. I probably have enough material for two more sequels! I cover several genres of music here, from the hard rockers in biker bars to the harmonious hymn-crooners of church choirs, from college symphonic orchestra to bluegrass wedding bands.

I started writing this in 2002 and have spent the last fourteen years adding stories whenever I found the time. Some were written as almost journalistic accounts, as they happened, while others happened years earlier. This explains some of the differences in age references, as well as references to people or events from a while back. Please note that even though I personally know and have access through my current work to many big names in the music business, none of the stories in this book are about the stars. They have their rewards. This is solely dedicated to and written about the guys and gals in the trenches.

All that said, if you are a musician, especially an old-timer, prepare yourself for a trip to a time you probably hold quite dear in your heart. If you are not a musician, just enjoy these stories, glimpses into the glamorous music business. If you were a musician in the seventies, you may discover a history of the wonderful time you had but were too stoned to remember. (On that note, please note that you will find very few stories about drugs, even though everyone knows they are a commonality of the music business. I'll even admit to my own involvement; unlike Bill Clinton, I *did* inhale. Even though I have some very funny stories involving drug use, I chose not to glamorize them in this book.)

So now I have just one more question for you: Are you ready to rock? Okay, then count it off...

A one, and a two, and a...!

Gigs from Down Under

(and I Don't Mean Australia)

House Band in a Whorehouse

In 1975, I played with Stonehenge, a hardcore rock 'n' roll band in the Cincinnati/northern Kentucky area. We were well known for our covers of Black Sabbath, Jimi Hendrix, and Blue Oyster Cult and had a good following in the local party crowd. The mid-seventies was a strange time for musicians because of disco music (and I use "music" very loosely here). Disco hit with an absolute vengeance, though, so as you can probably imagine, that left very few openings and gigs for hard rock 'n' roll. Everyone was expected to play "Shake Your Booty" or not play at all. I remember calling and visiting virtually every club and bar in town, pleading for a chance to take the stage; when we did get the chance, we always packed the house, no matter where it was. Nevertheless, the first question was always: "Are you a nine-piece horn band? If not, go away." We had many friends who went into country music just to avoid playing disco, and we even took on a couple country gigs ourselves just to make ends meet.

Somehow, one of the guys in the band landed us an audition at a place called the Riders Club. The venue was a bit strange, to say the least.

Sunday through Thursday, the club operated out of a small bar in the front of the building. On Friday and Saturday nights, the front bar was closed off with iron gates, and the so-called dance hall in the back was opened up; by that, I mean a place as big as a gymnasium, complete with a huge stage and a bar some forty feet long. The old man we presumed to be the club owner listened to a couple songs and offered us a gig as the house band, and we would be compensated with a nice salary and free beer. We later learned that the deed to the place was actually owned by a local politician with very questionable ties to the mob.

That gig seemed like a godsend to us: steady employment, plenty of brew, and no requirement to play disco or country. (On a side note, I have to mention that the free beer tab lasted only one weekend. The bartender advised us that we would only be granted half-price beer after that, because we drank way too much.) Since the back bar was closed all week, we could leave our gear, then set up and jam anytime we wanted. We were also free to play other one-night stands we had previously scheduled. All was perfect, or so we thought!

The first Friday night, we were pumped for the gig, our debut there, and we put on a fabulous show for four and a half hours for a grand total of three people. We were even more stunned when the waitress informed us that it was "the usual crowd." Sure, we were just dumb Kentucky boys, and musicians to boot, but even we figured out that something was not quite right with that picture. Saturday picked up a bit, as we entertained a whopping total of seven folks, three of which were our girlfriends. As the weeks progressed and word got out to our people about where we were playing, a real nice crowd began to show up. At the same time, we noticed that the bartender seemed more and more agitated the bigger the crowd got. We found that strange, too, considering that it meant he was selling more drinks.

Not long after we started playing at Riders, we began to notice some other odd behavior at the club. When we came in to play, for instance, there were always two guys standing by the iron gates at the front bar. Throughout the night, several men arrived and were let in through the gates and escorted through a door at the far end of the front bar. Later, several very well-dressed women were let in the same way, and the waitress carried trays of drinks in to them as the night progressed. This went on week after week. After we had been at the club for a couple months, we finally gained the confidence of the waitresses, and she told us what was really going on: Riders was actually a cover-up for an illegal gambling establishment and a house of ill repute, as some would call it. It only took us Kentucky boy musicians two months to figure it out. We also learned that the bartender's obvious worry was because we were drawing way too much attention to their little operation with the crowds we were pulling in.

In spite of all that, Stonehenge continued to play at the Riders Club for several more months, although I left the band eight or nine weeks after our first night. I actually drove by the old location of that club just the other day and saw that it is no longer there. Instead, the place is now home to a floral shop and parking lot.

We Play Both Kinds of Music Here, Country *and* Western

Anyone who has seen the classic movie *The Blues Brothers* can probably guess exactly what this story is about. As mentioned, my band Stonehenge was a hard rock band back in the mid-seventies, at the height of the disco era. It was harder for a hard rock band to find gigs during the reign of the Bee Gee's than it would be for Rush Limbaugh to book a keynote speaking spot at a National Organization of Women's convention! As a result, just to stay afloat, we had to play in some serious dives.

Our lead guitarist's family owned a campsite on Locust River in northeastern Kentucky, so one summer, we decided to spend a couple weeks there, writing and working on the show in the hopes of booking better gigs. We set up our equipment on the riverbank during the day and stored it in a large tent at night, which meant we took turns sleeping with our gear. While we were there, four young country girls arrived for a couple weeks of vacation at a log cabin just up the beach. They were absolute sweethearts and totally fascinated with the four longhaired, hard-drinking, pot smoking, rock 'n' roll musicians and became immediate groupies. Did I mention the thinnest girl in the bunch dressed out at about 300 pounds? Of course that didn't matter, as none of us were ever on the cover of *GQ;* besides, they had a shower in their cabin. We may have been freaks, but we were clean freaks and hated being dirty. We kept in contact with those girls for several years.

One day, we were on the beach jamming, and one of us started playing a country song. The rest of the band joined in, and before we were finished, some old dude came running out of his camper and stood in front of us, grinning from ear to ear. He immediately informed us that we just had to play for him at his bar several miles up the road. The name of the bar was Zeke's, no joke. Since we were broke and actually knew a couple country songs, we agreed. The way we saw it, country music was at least several rungs up the ladder from disco, so The Locust River Band was born. We spent the rest of the day working out some country tunes and were ready for Zeke's, or at least we thought we were.

As we drove up to Zeke's, we couldn't believe our eyes. The place looked like something straight out of a Jeff Foxworthy story. It sat high on a hill overlooking the river, with a long porch across the front that swaged in the middle by a good foot. Inside, Zeke's was packed with folks who had fewer teeth than third-shift at the average Waffle House. We set up and began playing, only to run out of songs within forty-five minutes, but the toothless crowd was nowhere near ready for us to quit playing. I started having visions of Ned Beatty in *Deliverance*. Luckily, three out of the four of us were born into families that loved country music, so we were at least familiar with a lot of country tunes. We did a pretty good job of winging it, and with that, coupled with many requests to replay certain songs, we survived and stretched the gig out until closing time. Believe it or not, by request, we played "Mama Tried" four times! At the end of the night, the owner handed us $200, something we didn't expect. Not only that, but with great excitement, he said, honest to God, "That's some of the best damn country music we've ever had in here."

Mind if We Dance with Yo' Dates?

Anyone who has played music for a living, to quote my son "back in the day", has played in some real dives. There's just no getting around it. No one starts out playing in stadiums or five-star hotels. I've always thought of it as paying your dues, and personally, I think it's a good thing, as it builds character and makes you appreciate the good gigs. I don't think musicians today have to go through what we did, but that's a discussion for another time, another book. Most of us survived the dives, and we all have some great stories to tell because of it. Among all those stories, I'm sure we can all remember one particular hole-in-the-wall, that place where you knew the moment you walked in that you were probably going to get your butt kicked, kind of like that scene in *Animal House* where the guys went to see Otis Day & the Knights, only to discover that they'd stepped into a blacks only establishment. "We're gonna die," Otter said, and I got that same feeling at McCoogin's Bar and Grill in eastern Kentucky.

McCoogin's was in a small river town, likely where Jeff Foxworthy got most of his material. I'll put it this way: There were far more tattoos than teeth in that town, and that was just counting the women! One local lady

showed up in the bar that night and actually bragged to our drummer that she

had "love" tattooed on her boob, and that was long before it was stylish for

women to get inked. Our drummer shared that with the bass player, Ronnie,

who proceeded to ask her if it was true. Ronnie was the kind of guy who liked

to stir stuff up whenever he got a chance, or maybe he was hoping she'd

show him. Anyway, she proudly proclaimed, in her finest Appalachian drawl,

"Honey, I got 'love' tattooed on my booby and 'danger' tattooed on my

p****y." That was the only time I ever saw Ronnie blush!

The owner of the club, whom we affectionately referred to as Old

Lady McCoogin, was short, about four feet tall and five feet wide. She was

also meaner than cat piss and took crap from absolutely no one. One night,

we saw her just flat out manhandle a drunk who had gotten out of control.

You need to get a mental picture of what "out of control" meant inside of

McCoogin's. Out of control was the usual modus operandi at this fine

establishment. I'm sure the S.W.A.T. team would have been called in at any

other redneck bar if the McCoogin's crowd showed up, but there, it was no

big thing. I'm sure you've seen bands playing behind chicken wire in the

movies, but that night, I was praying for steel bars. The only assurance we

had of surviving the gig was that most perturbed patrons usually leave the

band alone when it comes to bar fights. It also helped that our manager was

sitting at a table next to the stage, with a .357 Magnum lying in his lap, his hand firmly wrapped around the grip. Now that I think about it, I'm not sure if he had the pistol out to protect the band from the crowd or to protect himself from the band, since he was the one who set up the gig for us in the first place.

I'm still not sure what the drunk did to piss off Old Lady McCoogin, but I knew it wasn't good, and it probably would have easily earned him a five-to-ten bid in the big house. We were just coming off break when we heard some commotion at the far end of the bar. All of a sudden, the crowd parted like the Red Sea for Moses, and there stood the old lady, with one hand gripping the back of the drunk's collar and the other holding on to his belt. She violently dragged the guy across the dance floor, and he kicked and screamed all the way. She kicked open the exit door next to the stage and tossed this guy out, head first, right into the alley, then promptly turned to the crowd with an anyone-else-want-to-join-him? expression on her face. Of course there were no takers for her silent dare. She passed a glance over to us, the band, and her eyes asked, *"What the hell are you waiting for? Play somethin'."* We weren't about to mess with Old Lady McCoogin, especially while she was in killer mode, so we jumped into a song without even checking our tuning.

As you can imagine, the atmosphere kind of settled down after that. We finished the night without further incident, except for a slight run-in with a stringy-haired guy with green teeth who stood offstage left and yelled, "Hey, Rickey, play 'Tush'! C'mon! Play 'Tush'!"

They Couldn't Pay Us, but at Least They Made Up for It by Charging Us for Our Beer

I have played in some serious hole-in-the-wall joints, from those with chicken wire protection to the most redneck of the redneck bars, where we were sure we were destined to get our collective butts kicked. I've even played in a whorehouse, for crying out loud, but I just recently played in a joint that may win the prize for being the all-time worst dive ever. I even wrote a song about the place, "The Hole-in-the-Wall Blues." The Magnetic Café Club (MCC) is in Kent, Ohio, a hangout for the Goth crowd. There were some real scary people running around the place, some who looked more like pincushions than people. Actually, Kent itself seems to attract that dark and dismal crowd; on any given Friday, there's not a black shirt or pair of black pants to be found in any clothing stores within ten miles of Kent.

How I got the gig at The MCC is kind of interesting. I signed up for a program called Weekend Warriors at a local music store, started by the National Association of Music Manufacturers (NAMM). Through this program, musicians who haven't played in a while, or older new musicians, submit their names to a local music store. Bands are put together from the submitted names, based on interest, skill, and availability. By way of personal editorial, I submit that this is a most worthwhile program and a great way to meet other musicians, as well as a way to dust off your skills. Being a recent transplant to the Kent area, I took advantage of Warriors so I could hook up with some guys in a band. As part of the program, the bands play a gig at the end of a six-week session, so the music store set up The MCC gig for us.

When we found out where we would be playing, our two guitarists stopped by to check out the venue. They went into the owner's office to introduce themselves, and he promptly fired up a joint without even knowing who his guests were or whether or not they might be undercover cops. I talked to another musician who played at The MCC quite frequently, and he warned me about the crazy owner, who was well known for scheduling several bands to play at the same time. He always expected a couple bands to back out, and that was usually the case. From time to time, they all showed up, which made for an interesting evening. Bands played for free, and there were usually time slots for two each evening. This meant the second band carried their gear in through the front door and set it down on the dance floor while the first band played. When band one finished, it was pure pandemonium as they broke down their rig while band two set up theirs. To complicate matters even more, the venue had one of the smallest stages I'd ever seen. It was fine for a couple acoustic guitars or maybe a three-piece band, but it was a tight fit for our two guitars, bass, drums, and keyboard. For a PA, he actually had a couple nice cabinets, but he drove them with a guitar amp onstage and a small, cheap mixer with only four microphone inputs. We needed five mics, and since I work for a microphone manufacturer, I brought in a mic splitter to accommodate the extra one.

The club was dirty, none of the furnishing matched, and the restroom smelled awful. I had to make a note to myself to bring my own toilet paper next time, since there wasn't so much as a sheet of it in there. The facilities at The MCC actually ranked lower than the john you'd find in a back-alley auto shop. To put it mildly, it was gross. One interesting highlight was that handbills were tacked or taped all over the walls, bearing extremely liberal political cartoons and ads. For example, one depicted George Bush bending over another president, who was bending over another, doing something real nasty. There was other Perez-Hilton-gone-over-the-rainbow-to-visit-Dorothy-type literature prominently displayed on tables at the entrance. Suffice it to say these five Reagan Conservative musicians felt more than a little out of place there.

The owner/bartender would wait to gauge how big his crowd might be, then ran to the grocery store to buy beer. The barmaid was dumb as a sack of hammers and slow as a postal worker on Thorazine.

One would think that once we finished the gig, The MCC would fade away into our archives of bad memories, especially after they charged us for beer. We provided an evening of free entertainment, so it seemed only right that he would give us beer, but he even charged me for a bottle of water. Nevertheless, instead of The MCC becoming a bad memory, we became regulars on their stage. Now I have to wonder who was crazier, the owner or us.

How About a Camel?

Every musician has dreams. Some dream of making it big, with gold records and tons of money, a chance to live the rock star lifestyle. Others dream or, more accurately, have nightmares of falling flat on their faces with no money, screwed over by management or labels, and ending up playing dives, entertaining roomfuls of sloppy drunks who aren't even paying attention. Have you ever dreamt that you were playing for animals or, even worse, *with* animals? You might say, "Well, maybe after a real long gig with lots of booze, followed by a trip to an all night chili parlor." For Matthias and his band, Words of the Prophet, it was far more than a dream; for them, it was a reality.

Words of the Prophet was a very unique, Christian rock band with plenty of drive and lots of substance. Most of their music was written by Matthias, a jazz guitar college major whose influences ranged from seventies rock and blues to U2, from Dan Fogelberg to swing/big band. Words of the Prophet was a four-piece band with two very good lead guitarists, and their excellent vocalists brought three-part harmony to many of their songs. Their

style was often compared to Creed, with just a touch of jazz and better vocals.

The band was booked to play at a weekend Christian music festival in

rural eastern Ohio, at a county fairground. The facility was actually quite nice,

with a huge stage, lots of seating, and plenty of parking. Not unusual for that

type of festival, security was provided by a Christian motorcycle gang. Even

though they were generally very nice guys, they didn't look it, so I was sure

the crowd would behave and wouldn't be an issue. All the other bands and

most of the audience were head-banger types, but that wasn't Words of the

Prophet.

All day long, band after band took the stage, with guitarists who

played nothing but power chords, with nary-a-lead solo in earshot. The bass

players only needed the E-string, with a heavy pick for playing just the root

note. All the drummers played like they were pissed at something, their veins

popping in their temples and forearms while they left a pile of splinters and

sawdust from stray, purportedly accidental rim-shots. The vocals were a cross

between the demon's in *The Exorcist* and the screeches of excited fans at a

hockey game. Trying very hard not to show my age, I can honestly say no one

could tell when one band left the stage and another took over. Most had

some kind of gimmick, such as the drummer facing backward or the lead

singer running around in circles, kicking over mic stands or drums, all staged

for that purpose, but not one really stood out. They weren't good showmen, and most were oblivious to the fact that they even had an audience. The crowd appeared to reciprocate by paying very little attention to most of the bands, which was odd since they paid to get in!

In the midst of that madness, Words of the Prophet took the stage and dared to start their set with prayer, as it was supposed to be a Christian event. They proceeded into a rocking tune with harmonized lead guitar parts, three-part vocal harmony, and a stage show that was worth the price of admission. What a performance they gave! The other bands looked on in amazement, and one bass player even whined, "No fair! They have two lead guitarists, and we don't even have one!"

I really just told you that story to set the stage for another. See, one of the guitarists from Words of the Prophet knew the festival organizers quite well and volunteered the band to help out with some of the logistics, such as managing the stage crew and working with the sound company. The band arrived a day early to help with setup. Loudspeakers had to be hoisted, snakes had to be run, and all the other normal activities associated with a concert had to be completed. At one point during the morning, Matthias went into the green room backstage. When he opened the curtain that led offstage left, he found himself nose to nose with a camel, a real, live one, humps and all. Matthias wasn't exactly the outdoors type, so, needless to say, he freaked out. Also, being a politically conservative individual during a time of war with a Middle Eastern country, it was highly likely that he feared terrorists might have landed at the fairground, with plans to shut down the Christian concert. Actually, to Matthias's credit, it would have probably startled Marlin Perkins, since it was so out of place; no one would expect to have a stare-down with a camel on just any old day.

You might be wondering how such a beast came to be at a Christian concert. Apparently, some small, rural towns are not very organized, or perhaps they are a bit too relaxed when scheduling events. In this case, they had double-booked the concert and a circus at the fairgrounds. They were able to separate the two events into different areas, but the circus folks thought the arena would be a marvelous place for the animals to stretch their legs. When the circus people realized the arena was actually being used, they quickly removed the animals. After seeing some of the acts that went on that day, though, I didn't think separating them was necessary. I doubt anyone would have noticed.

Dayton Music Fest: Screwed Over by the Pros

Every band dreams of the opportunity to open for a touring national act. When you are the opening act, it means you're on your way. Case in point: Jimi Hendrix opened for The Monkees! While playing with the Almost Ready for Divine Time Players (ARFDTP), I had just such an opportunity. The ARFDTP was a band and vocal group born out of the Promise Keepers movement of the 1990s. We were comprised of a fantastic band of old rockers who used to play in clubs, along with twenty-two talented male singers. Our set list was comprised of mostly Promise Keepers tunes, with a few other great Christian rock and contemporary songs thrown in. The band started out playing for church men's groups, then moved on to conferences, with the occasional stadium gig.

There was one thing about the guys in that band: It did not matter where it was or how big or small the venue or crowd was, they were ready to play. For several of those gigs, the band outnumbered the audience, but they didn't care. I, on the other hand did care, not from a performance standpoint but from the one of logistics. My main role, besides lead vocals and bass guitar, was to serve as band director. I also owned most of the equipment. So, by default, I was in charge of the haul-in, setup, and load-out of the gear. It was no problem for the vocalists to travel 200 miles and walk onstage just in time for sound check and to play for twenty guys, but it was a different story for us band guys. We had to tear down our stuff from the practice site, load it into a rented truck, trailer, or several vans, then drive to the site, set up, and play. By performance time, we were usually sweaty and dirty, and then we had to do the same thing in reverse, all over again. It may sound like I'm complaining here, but I'm very happy to finally get that off my chest! Now that I'm finished whining, I can move on to the story.

We received an offer we could not refuse, one that was simply too good to be true, to play as the opening act for a couple well-known recording artists at an outdoor Christian music festival in Dayton, Ohio. To make the deal even sweeter, a local radio station planned to air a live program during the show and asked to interview us and air our set. We were sure that was it, that we were on our way.

I started working with the radio station months ahead of time, to inform them of our stage needs, and the radio station worked with the concert organizers to organize the sound system. The setup was kind of weird: The main talent would play on the main stage while we set up in front of it. The sound system setup was just as odd: The radio station intended to mix us on their console, then send a feed to the front of house console to go out over the main speakers. It was completely backward from the usual, but beggars couldn't be choosy, so we were in no position to argue.

We got there hours early and set up in the blistering sun of late July. After that, we were informed by the concert organizers that we could not check sound until the main act finished their checks. We sat their waiting for the longest time, but they finally arrived, forty-five minutes late, and ran their sound check for more than thirty minutes over their allotted time. We could only look on in horror as they moped around the stage, taking their sweet time—and ours—joking with each other and doing everything but checking sound. All the while, airtime was fast approaching. They finally finished and went into their trailer right at airtime, so we went out live over the airways and through the PA system with no sound check.

Our sound was awful, as you might imagine, not only on the radio but also blaring from the main speakers. To make matters even more embarrassing, by that time, several thousand people had arrived and were blasted with the mass of offensive noise coming out of the mains. I looked over at the radio engineer and saw him frantically twisting knobs and sliding faders, trying to get a mix, looking as terrified as a whore in church. We played a total of five tunes, but it took the engineer until the end of the third before he arrived at a mix that sounded even remotely like a band was playing, versus a twenty-minute train wreck. I can honestly say it was the most humiliating musical moment of my career. We didn't even stick around to hear the other bands play; we just tore down and loaded our gear in record time. We did get a bit of final satisfaction from the headliners, though, perhaps a little divine intervention, because a huge lighting storm assaulted them with high winds and flooding rain right in the middle of their first song, forcing them to cancel the show.

Musicians, Strippers, Hamburgers, and Chili

I've been writing a lot about the not-so-glamorous side of the music business, bad gigs, equipment failure, getting ripped off by club owners, and so on. These are essential events in the life of every musician, as they help to build character, as well as provide great stories for the bar—or books like this one. Although not all of these tales are necessarily glamorous, not all are particularly bad. In particular, I consider the events that take place right after the gig, the stuff that happens when the crowd has gone and the gear is safely packed way in the van. Jackson Browne included a great song about this very subject on his *Running on Empty* album, a tune called "The Load-Out." Few of us ever reach the level of 20,000 fans and a crew of roadies, so here, I'm talking about the guys who haul in their own stuff, play the gig, then break it all down again with their own two hands. What happens when the music stops but the kick drum is still pounding in your head, you're still wide awake, and everything is closed? For musicians in the northern Kentucky/Cincinnati area at that time, what happened involved chili or hamburgers.

There are a couple things you need to know about Newport, Kentucky in the 1970s. The place was a bit on the shady side and had been for years. No, that's putting it lightly. Actually, it was really sleazy, fraught with countless strip clubs, along with prostitution and illegal gambling houses. Organized crime was well established in the town. As I mentioned earlier in "House Band in a Whorehouse," I even played in an illegal gambling casinos and home for wayward girls. Today, Newport is quite different. It has been cleaned up and revitalized and is currently a very nice place to live or do business, but back then, a guy could get laid, lose his money, and get his butt kicked all in one night.

Anyway, after the gig, bands were typically on the road by around three or four a.m., feeling hungry, buzzed, and ready for anything but sleep. Since most everything was closed at that hour, there were only two choices, Dixie Chili or White Castle hamburgers, both of which stayed open all night. Since all the bars and strip clubs closed at the same time, countless strippers, prostitutes, and musicians all descended on one of these two establishments. What a sight it was, all those longhaired, hippie-type, stoned musicians and acres of T&A! There were occasional hookups, of course, but that wasn't the norm; on a musician's salary, it just wasn't possible. Usually, it was just a bunch of crazy people enjoying each other's company, trying to sober up while scarfing down chili and sliders. For those who have missed out on these delights, Cincinnati-style chili is a very thin, watery version of the soup, typically served over spaghetti—known as a three-way when it includes cheese; a four-way with kidney beans, or a five-way when onions are added. White Castle is famous for sliders, little square, grilled hamburgers with diced onions, served on steamed buns. The best part was that back then, sliders cost next to nothing. True to their name, while they are the tastiest thing on the planet, they are potent as hell and slide right through anyone who eats them. For this reason, they were—and still are—more affectionately referred to as rectum rockets, for obvious reasons. White Castle also offers some of the best coffee around, served in cups that keep it hot for hours. I always swore I would insulate my house with ground up White Castle coffee cups.

Just a couple years ago, a very good friend of mine and the best drummer I've ever jammed with, Jack Snow, tied the knot. Most of the people on the guest list were musicians from back in the day. The joke was on them when the meal was catered by none other than White Castle!

Battle of the Blands

Have you ever participated in a Battle of the Bands or at least attended one? If you have ever participated in or witnessed one of these contests, do you think the best band actually won? My guess would be probably not. Most likely, you stood there in stunned amazement as the absolutely smokin' band received fourth place at best, while some no-talent, head-banging punk group walked away with top honors. That always drives me crazy, but how does it happen? Are the contests fixed? Do the judges have their heads up somebody's poop shoot? Or is it possible that the winning bands actually do have something, a talent you somehow missed, that special *je ne sais quoi?* No way! If there is one thing I can guarantee, it is that the best bands rarely win a Battle of the Bands. Please note that I said "rarely" though. Why? Because I actually had the honor of judging the finals of a Battle of the Bands in Kent, Ohio; in that case, I can assure you that the best band won. Am I claiming I'm a better judge than anyone else? Not at all! I just so happened to be on a panel of five judges that day, but the order I predicted was exactly how those bands finished in the contest. What was the difference? I'll give you my opinion in a moment, but first, let me share a story about a very disappointing finish to a battle one of my friend's bands competed in.

Matthias is a very talented singer, songwriter, and musician, usually the front man for whatever band he plays with. Anyone who watches him perform for a moment will clearly see why this is the case. At one time, Matthias hooked up with an established band comprised of fantastic musicians with very strong vocal abilities. The band was looking for a lead guitarist, and it just so happened that my friend had just left a band that had dissolved over some tough internal strife. It was the perfect opportunity for Matthias at the perfect time, because he wanted to just play, without being the star. Not only that, but it was a much disciplined, mature group of musicians who had already released several CDs, and one of their songs was actually climbing the Christian charts in some markets. After a couple months, with several shows behind them, they entered a Battle of the Bands in Cincinnati, one I attended with several of my other friends. The contest hosted several fine bands, but as is typically the case, I really couldn't figure out how a couple of them made it to the finale.

Matthias's band walked onstage, a tight group who offered good old rock 'n' roll with a touch of sophistication. Their vocal harmonies were simply amazing. Of course, since they actually started years earlier as an acapella vocal group, it was no wonder their vocals were so nice. They were all very good showmen, although I must admit that Matthias's stage presence still shone through, even when he wasn't the man up front. It wasn't at all surprising that they finished the set to a great audience response, and I was glad I'd invited friends to the awesome performance.

The bands that followed Matthias seemed more like circus acts. Every one of them relied on some kind of unnecessary gimmick, things that actually detracted from their music; then again, for several of those bands, that was actually a good thing. The band that ultimately won was, without a doubt, the weirdest and least talented of the bunch, but there were likely a couple reasons that they took home the prize. First, they had a huge following, and they'd brought their fans with them; there was plenty of screaming, clapping, and yelling throughout their performance, giving the illusion that they were better than they actually were. Second, and probably the most important reason, the judging was done by the front-of-house (FOH) engineer, a known head-banger who just so happened to be very good friends with the band. It wasn't exactly fixed, but that judging arrangement made it very difficult for the other competing bands. Matthias's band was clearly the most talented of the bunch, with the best music selection, but under those conditions, they had absolutely no chance of winning and only placed a disgraceful fifth.

Fair judging for a Battle of the Bands can be a matter of opinion, but the contest I judged underwent one of the best process I've ever witnessed.

First, the five judges were all from different walks of life, with various backgrounds in different music styles. Second, none of us had seen any of the bands in the preliminary competition, so they were fresh to us, and we had no preconceived ideas about them. Finally, the bands were judged on several criteria, including originality, stage presence, audience engagement, and overall performance. I actually had to give high scores to some bands that played music I did not like because they played it so well and scored high in other areas.

Is there a moral to this story, something you can take with you to your next competition? Probably not. When it comes to a Battle of the Bands, you will likely have no idea what kind of judging you'll be subject to. If winning is extremely important to you, you might be able to dig up a little information on the judging process and the judges beforehand, then let that determine if you will change your show or if you will participate at all. Other than that, I just encourage you to show up and play what you want to play, to the best of your ability. Why? Because no matter where you place in what might very well be a Battle of the Blands, it will be another opportunity to show your stuff in front of a larger crowd than usual. You may actually land a few gigs out of the experience, as well as make contacts with some other musicians or industry moguls who can help you along in your career.

Hillbillies Love It in the Hay

From time to time, all musicians are asked to play a gig that falls a bit outside their style or comfort zone. I've always counseled younger musicians, including my son, that these gigs are good for you, for a number for reasons. First, it's always best to be the worst musician in the band rather than the star; this is almost always the case when I play. Sure, the star looks good and might get all the chicks, but that person doesn't learn much or have much room for improvement. When everyone else is better than you, not only do you have to stretch yourself, but you can also pick up something from the other guys. The same thing applies to playing styles and venues outside your norm. Just think of the great music that has been created by fusing different styles. Again, nothing ventured, nothing gained! If you refuse to play nothing but eighties hair band music, for instance, you can count on finding your CDs on the dollar rack at Walmart. Finally, money is a good thing. If they are paying good bucks at the polka barn and you're broke, well, it kinda sounds like a no-brainer to me.

I had the opportunity to play a gig that both stretched me musically and pulled me way out of my style. I had met a young fiddler while playing in a church service. The music director had arranged a laidback program for a particular Sunday service and asked if I would play the upright bass for him, even though I usually play six-string electric bass. During the week following the service, the fiddle player called me and asked if I would be willing play upright at a wedding with him and some pickers in central Kentucky, because the couple wanted a bluegrass band to play during the ceremony. I really wasn't good enough to play doghouse bass with professional Nashville musicians, and I've never really cared much for bluegrass music, but I still agreed to do the gig, precisely for all the reasons I mentioned above. In the end, it turned out to be a real hoot, and I met some great musicians.

Before I describe this wedding, I must say up front that I don't expect any of you to believe this story. Even as I write it, I know it sounds like I'm making it up, but it actually happened. As I mentioned, they wanted all the songs before and during the ceremony to be bluegrass. Although I had never played the tunes, I had heard most of them, so I decided to just ride one and five with an occasional run and let the real players carry the tune. The bride would walk in to "Canon in D," but, honest to God, they asked if we could "make it sound bluegrass." I'm sorry, but some things are just too sacred to mess with; you should have seen the looks I received when I pulled out a bow for the tune!

The wedding was held at the bride's family farm, a gorgeous place. It was set up on a slight hill, with about twenty rows of hay bales positioned in a semicircle, facing a lake. It was great fun watching some of the ladies being torturously poked with straw as they attempted to sit on those bales in their short, fancy dresses and nylons! The band was situated off to the side of the wedding party, directly in the late July sun, so hot and bright that as a reward, I received a terrible case of sunburn on my bald spot. The mothers were supposed to walk in to a bluegrass rendition of "Wind Beneath My Wings." The wedding coordinator gave us the go-ahead with a nod, and we started the song. After about ten verses, we discovered that the bride's mother was nowhere to be found; it turned out that she was in the house peeling potatoes and had missed her cue. Once the mothers were finally seated, after what seemed like ten more verses, and with the wedding party down front, the bride, a major babe in her own right, arrived atop the fender of John Deere tractor, with her father behind the wheel. Lord, smack me down if I'm lying!

We played a couple tunes during the ceremony, including a song that would have traditionally been played during the lighting of the unity candle; it was a bit too windy for flames, so they planted a tree instead. The groom had a friend who had learned three chords and had written a country love song for the couple. I didn't catch his name, but I would not have been surprised to find out it was Bubba. After the I-do's, the pastor pronounced them husband and wife, and they marched down the aisle to none other than

"Foggy Mountain Breakdown!" The husband placed his bride back on the tractor, then climbed behind the wheel and drove down the lane.

We continued playing bluegrass tunes, getting redder and redder beneath the baking, unforgiving sun, as the crowd very slowly dissipated, still picking bits of hay out of their nooks and crannies. Finally, when only a couple stragglers were left, the coordinator came by and paid us, and we headed home.

How Many Guys Are in This Band?

I very seriously doubt this event could have happened anywhere but in a church environment, because most musicians outside a church would never stand for it. Before I dive into the tale, I'd like to mention the many things church musicians put up with that the guys who play bar gigs would never, ever tolerate.

First, churches typically have on staff one individual who calls all the shots, even though that particular person may not have a clue. I'm referring here to the worship leader. Don't get me wrong: There are some great ones out there, but a large number of them are really just kids who've never played in a real band. Of course that inexperience does not stop them from telling a bass player who's been on tour for twenty-five years, "Just simplify." I once played in a church band that brought in a visiting worship leader for a weeklong series of services, and the guy was a real doofus. The band consisted of old rockers with ten or twelve albums between them, yet the jerk insisted on telling all the guys when and how to play. By the end of the week, he had lost most of the band and ended up leading via piano alone; then again, I think that was what he really wanted in the first place. Many worship leaders are also in charge of the sound system, as well as the sound engineers. Even if they don't know the difference between a fader and a dipstick, their lack of knowledge doesn't stop them from constantly barking out orders to the sound guy.

Outside the typical issues with the worship leader, it also seems most congregants feel they have the right to tell the band members what's wrong with their playing. In my forty years of playing clubs, I can honestly say I've never once been approached by a bar patron who told me I was too loud or that my dancing onstage was way too provocative. Honest to God, I've been told by certain churchgoers that my moving around onstage was offensive! I confess that I do sometimes look like I'm ready to turn backflips off my amp at any moment, but that's just the way I play, and it is not the business of any old, blue-haired church lady. After all, the Bible talks about King David dancing before the Lord, and we all know bass players dance, so I personally like to think I'm just following the Good Book! I once knew a guitar player who was jumped all over by a group of Pentecostal women because they felt the shape of his guitar was satanic, as they put it. Of course, for a guy in a bar, that would have been a compliment, especially when playing Sabbath.

I think the most challenging thing church musicians face is that darn near everything they want to do may be offensive to one or more individuals on the church staff or in the congregation. Never mind the fact that Sister

Suzanne has no problem offending the drummer by ripping him a new one

because he's too loud, stating that the band has to be "attentive to the needs

of the congregation." Give me a break! To be honest, it's a good thing

musicians are there to use their gifts to glorify God; otherwise, those cats

would be back in the clubs in a heartbeat.

Now, with apologies for that little tirade, I will get back to my

original thought. Jonathan was a Pentecostal worship leader; by

"Pentecostal," I mean old-line, slain-in-the-Spirit, tongues-talking, shouting,

laying-on-of-hands, running-around-the-church, and frothing-at-the-mouth

Pentecostal. He was only about half a step from snake handling, though I

can't say for sure that he didn't indulge in that too. He was also one of the

best piano players I've ever heard. He played the Jimmy Swaggart/Jerry Lee

Lewis style of Southern gospel most of the time, though I'm sure he could

have played just about anything. I once heard him sing and play a Christian

parity of Billy Joel's "Piano Man," and he simply burned up the keys!

Jonathan was also one of the nicest guys on the planet, a good ol' boy adored

by everyone. Of course, that very personality trait is the kind of thing that can

cause a musician a whole lot of trouble in certain circles.

I met Jonathan during the early days of the Promise Keepers

crusades and started playing bass for him at men's rallies. We got our band

together and practiced a couple times before the rallies, and we actually

poured out some pretty great sound. The band usually consisted of Jonathan on keys, my good friend Jack Snow on drums, a guitar player to be named later, and me on bass. All seemed fine at practice, but the problems reared their ugly heads at gigs. We showed up, only to find out that Jonathan had invited several other musicians to sit in, sometimes doubling up on instruments. Of course those guys didn't know the tunes, which was a problem in itself, but even worse, it's just not practical to have two bass players and three drummers during the same song. I was very surprised at how bad some of them were, considering how good Jonathan was by comparison.

One gig that comes to mind was actually a fairly big deal. We had been asked to play at a commissioning service the night before a major Promise Keepers crusade, and they were expecting about 2,000 to be in attendance. Jack Snow and I arrived early to set up. Over the next half-hour, ten or twelve additional musicians showed up, ready to play. We ended up with several keyboardists, an assortment of horns, a couple guitarists, and a percussionist or two, who mistakenly thought *they* were going to be drumming. Another bass player showed up, but when he saw me and my rig, he promptly backed out. As each musician arrived, they advised us that Jonathan had invited them to sit in.

I looked at Jack in disgust and asked, "Just how is this supposed to work? These guys don't know the tunes or our arrangements. I predict a major train wreck here!"

Being the sensible guy he was, Jack replied, "Hey, we're on the other side of town, and no one knows us here. When it all goes to hell in a handbasket, just duck your head and sneak out the back door. We'll never see any of these people again anyway."

It was really good advice from a great friend. I was actually quite shocked at how well the event went, although afterward, I reamed Jonathan for continually doing that to us. I felt real guilty about jumping on him, though, because he looked at me as if I'd just kicked his dog. In any case, I guess I got through to him, because from that point on, we didn't have to worry about a pack of musicians showing up.

I've heard horror stories from other church musicians who have experienced similar situations. I am perplexed at why church worship leaders and pastors think it is perfectly all right for them to invite people off the street to sit in. Without hesitation, I can tell you that I've never once walked into a bar gig and found that the bartender had invited an extra marimba player. I can also assure you that if that did ever happen, the band would likely turn right around and walk out, and I wouldn't blame them one bit!

Saturday Night's All Right for Fighting

Great local musician stories unfold just about anywhere in the world, not just here in the U.S. I met a musician from eastern Canada at a trade show in Las Vegas, and he told me a great story about a club he used to play in back in the early seventies. Mick played guitar in a local rock band, and by his own humble description, they "weren't bad." In fact, he said they actually had a decent following who faithfully showed up at most of their gigs. I'm not at all familiar with the Canadian music scene, though I would like to thank them for sending us Rush! I also know next to nothing about the socioeconomics of the Canucks, so I hope to give at least a partially accurate account of his story here.

According to Mick, he played in one town quite frequently, a place where farming was the main way of life. During harvest time, the population swelled with migrant farm workers. On the weekends, after working hard in the fields all week, they were ready to party; in other words, they were eager to drink, fight, chase women, dance, drink, and fight some more. Did I mention drink and fight? Anyway, I think you get the picture. Evidently, the town had very strict occupancy laws, so even though the club was about as large as a small gymnasium, there was always a line of people waiting to get in. The bouncer at the door did his best to keep the peace and enforce the occupancy rules, and there was also someone there to collect cover charges.

Musicians have a very unique vantage point from the stage, and we get to see a lot of things the general population misses out on. Most people think the show happens onstage and the audience is there to watch, but in reality, the most entertaining thing is what happens out on the floor, something only the band is privy to. You would not believe the things I've seen playing in bars, dance clubs, and stadiums, even on church platforms! It's enough to write a book.

Anyway, from behind the microphone, Mick could always spy that one group of rabble-rousers who were in the place just to start a fight. He watched as they strutted through the crowd like roosters in the barnyard, with their chests puffed out, their chins held high, and smug looks on their faces that said, *"That's right! I'm bad, and I'm about to kick somebody's behind."* Soon, a suitable victim would be found, and the pissing contest would commence; this always resulted in chairs flying through the air, tables being busted and broken, glasses and mugs being shattered, and noses being bloodied. Within seconds, the team of bouncers, all of whom expected it to happen anyway, descended on the scene like a S.W.A.T. team, and they made quick work of throwing the brawl participants out quite forcibly.

Bar fights happen all the time, so this story may not seem all that unusual. What makes it unique is what happened *after* the fight. According to Mick, those who were tossed out would get back in line at the front door and wait their turn, pay another cover charge, and reenter the establishment, only to repeat the process again. By way of editorial comment, I would like to add a great quote from *Animal House*: "Fat, drunk, stupid [and redneck] is no way to go through life, son."

Can You Really Die of Embarrassment?

I've often heard people say, "I was so embarrassed that I coulda just died!" If you're anything like me, you've probably said that a time or two yourself. If you are a parent who dares to take your children out in public, I'm sure it is a common occurrence for you. It makes one wonder if it is truly possible to actually give up the ghost, take a dirt nap, sleep with the daises, or gasp your last breath due to nothing more than humiliation. I'm not even counting those times when someone is caught with their hand in the cookie jar and jumps out a window. Can the heart really stop beating due to the emotional stress of embarrassment? Just imagine that: One minute, a guy is laughing and joking with his friends while watching a ballgame, and in the next, he finds himself standing at the pearly gates because his wife asked if she could borrow his black bra and panty set. Maybe that's a bad example, since that guy's friends would likely beat him to death before the embarrassment would even have a chance to do more than redden his cheeks. In any case, I'm not a doctor, so I can't say for sure if one can die from humiliation, but I have suffered through an experience that carried me pretty darn close to finding out.

Several years ago, I was the band leader for a men's choral group called The Almost Ready for Divine Times Players, which I briefly mentioned before. I co-led the group with a man named Sam, the front man of the group. He was perfect for that role, because he was energetic, very likeable, well spoken, and extremely corny. Sam was also an excellent vocal director, although he himself did not necessarily possess a very good voice. He was okay when singing as part of an ensemble, but he really wasn't worthy of solos. Most of our tunes were written for ensemble or choir, so we thought all was well. The group did include some tremendous soloists, and Sam was thrilled to let those talented guys handle the few songs that called for solo voices.

We were asked to perform at a large African Methodist Episcopal church that was quite well known for their music program, both band and choir. It did not take long for us to learn firsthand that their reputation was well earned. Their music director was the band director at a very large, prestigious high school, and he also performed in local jazz clubs. He accompanied the choir sitting behind a Hammond B3, with two Leslie tone cabinets, and boy, did he make that thing talk! After sitting in with us on only a couple tunes, it already sounded as if he'd been playing with us for years. Still, as great as the keyboardist was, he paled in comparison to the vocalists.

Several of the female singers sang solos, and I was absolutely floored; it was like an entire choir of Aretha Franklin clones, absolutely amazing.

That outstanding choir opened the show, so I was a bit intimidated as we took the stage; it was the proverbial hard act to follow. Nevertheless, it turned out to be one of our best performances ever. When we played, the church choir remained seated behind us in their loft, and throughout our performance, the ladies seated right behind us kept shouting, "Yeah! You go on now! That's how you play it!" That really fired me up and inspired me to play all the better. I've always been known for dancing a little, and that encouragement sure got my feet moving and even added a few more moves to my strut, and the rest of the group was affected in much the same way. It is so nice when the crowd is into it and the band is on, a great combination indeed!

We finished the set to great accolades, and everyone sat down except Sam. I figured he was just going to make some sort of announcement about future gigs or thank the church for asking us to play, but instead, he informed everyone that he was going to perform a solo. *"Please, God, don't let this happen,"* I prayed, almost aloud, but my prayer was too late.

Sam had given an accompaniment tape to the sound guy before the concert, and that music started playing. I don't remember the song, but I do remember that it was entirely out of his range and sounded absolutely awful. *Sam, you idiot,* I thought. *What are you thinking? You just heard those ladies sing like angels, and our performance was way over our heads. Why do you have to ruin it? You know you can't sing!* I looked around at the other guys in the band, and they all had their heads down, with their eyes glued to the floor, just as humiliated as I was. Like me, they were all suffering from utter and complete embarrassment, the kind no mortal should ever have to endure, all desperately trying to think of some way to escape the hell we'd suddenly been thrown into right there in a church. It wouldn't have surprised me if one of them would have sneaked out into the hall and pulled the fire alarm, just to give us an easy escape from our plight. As Sam crooned away, I thought for sure the ladies in the choir were going to burst out in laughter at any moment, but those sweet women had too much class to do such a thing, and they even graciously managed to offer a modest amount of applause when he finished his audible, off-key assault.

Pryor to that fiasco of a performance, I was looking forward to meeting the other musicians. Instead, I hid in the bathroom for ample time to allow the crowd to leave. Needless to say, everyone in the group gave Sam a piece of their minds and informed him that he would not be singing any more unannounced solos in the future.

Asleep at the Wheel

Everyone suffers embarrassing events now and then, those moments when we would love to crawl up under our hats and disappear from the world. Then there are those extraordinary, sometimes colossal moments that seem to define and label us for the rest of our lives. I'm sure you know what I mean. For example, someone may ask, "Hey, do you remember Joey from junior high?" Even though this Joey is now the president and CEO of some Fortune 500 company, has written several bestsellers, and has more money than Michael Jackson's attorney, you just can't seem to place him until someone says, "You know Joey, that kid who got drunk for the first time at Sally Martin's birthday party and pooped his pants." Only then does it click, and you suddenly blurt, "Oh yeah! I remember Stinky!" Truly, once a label is inflicted upon us, particularly when tied to an embarrassing event, that label can seldom be removed. No matter how successful you are, how much money you make, or how many folks you knock off from your past, there will always be someone who remembers and is all too happy to tell the story again and again and again, probably exacerbating the problem by exaggerating the most embarrassing details more with each retelling, like that telephone game we all played in kindergarten.

One thing that makes these embarrassing moments even worse is the fact that most of the time, they are self-inflicted. Sure, sometimes stuff just happens that is totally and completely out of our control, but those circumstantial events are usually forgotten. The things that really nail us, really stick are those numb-nuts, brain-cramp, lost-touch-with-reality, what-the-hell-was-I-thinking? moments we can never seem to get rid of.

Speaking of numb nuts, I will now share one of the numbest-nutted events I've ever heard of concerning a very talented musician I've already mentioned, Mathias, that singer/songwriter who plays several instruments extremely well. I engineered one of his CDs, and he played all the instruments on it, including guitars, drums, piano, keyboards, bass, mandolin, saxophone, flute, and harmonica; he also remarkably handled all the vocals. Mathias plays just about any instrument on the planet extremely well, and I believe he's the best tenor sax man I've ever met. He toured with several bands before striking out on his own, and he shared the following story with me from his college days.

Matthias was a music major at Northern Kentucky University (NKU), and during his freshman year, part of his curriculum required him to play in the symphonic band. That particular band always played for the graduation ceremony, and attendance was required for all band members in order for them to receive a grade in the class. That year, commencement would be held in downtown Cincinnati, at Riverfront Coliseum, the hockey rink where many big concerts take place. In other words, there was plenty of room for a large crowd. The place is quite famous, due to a most unfortunate event that occurred there during The Who concert back in the seventies, but I digress.

NKU contracted with a local bus company to pick the band members up at six a.m. at the school, then shuttle them to and from the Coliseum. This was where Matthias's numb-nuts decision came in. Now, we've all heard it said that most talented musicians are right-brained, and Matthias is an extreme case in point. Let me explain: He is pure magic onstage, provided he remembers that he's supposed to be onstage for a gig, as well as when and where that gig is and what he's supposed to bring, such as guitar, amp, cables, saxophone, and so on. Truly, Matthias must have a manager or personal secretary to look out for him at all times. While he was in school, his parents were aware of this shortcoming, and they made sure to provide such a service for him and to manage his calendar well, so their prodigy did not miss any important assignments or opportunities. During this particular performance, however, his parents were out of town on vacation, unavailable for powdering his butt and putting it on that bus. Realizing that missing the event would cost him a semester grade and that there was no possible way he would wake up on his own, Matthias came up with a quick solution: He would just stay up all night, to avoid any chance of sleeping in.

Surprisingly, he actually made it to the bus on time and arrived at the gig intact, dressed, and with saxophone in hand. The stage was set up with a podium in the middle for the speaker, and the band was to play in front of the podium. The event would be broadcast on the jumbotron screens to allow everyone in the Coliseum to see what was happening onstage. Matthias was situated center stage, directly in front of the podium; that would normally be considered a great seat, but that was certainly not the case for this performance. He did not realize the effect his forced insomnia would have on him, particularly because he had to now sit on a hot stage, dressed in a black tuxedo, listening to several long, boring speeches. As is probably obvious, he was out cold in a matter of minutes.

Matthias's impromptu siesta might not have been so bad, except that he was positioned directly between the camera and the university president. There he was, with his head lolled back, his mouth wide open, his arms spread wide, and bigger than life on the jumbotron! The crowd began to giggle, the rest of the band started snickering and cracking up, and the band director was about ready to have the proverbial fit. One would think Matthias's friends, his comrades, his fellow band members would have thought enough of him to gently nudge him awake and save him from such impending embarrassment, but they were college students, some of whom seemed to be seeking a degree in public humiliation, the kind of classmates who made hazing so popular. Thus, they just sat idly by and let Matthias continue his humiliating snooze-fest.

The cameraman finally adjusted his angle enough to cut the sleeping musician out of the shot, but the damage was already done. To this day, most students do not remember Matthias until someone says, "You know, that guy we called Sleepy!"

The Camp Springs Occult Blues Band

I grew up in a very small town that could barely pass as a town at all. We did have a general store, a place so small that the sales clerk retrieved all the items for shoppers. We also had one gas station, a Fire Department, one church, and four bars; priorities, I suppose. Regardless of the fact that it was not exactly a thriving metropolis, Camp Springs covered a lot of geographical area, about twenty square miles, and people who lived thirty minutes away from me still claimed it as their hometown.

The area was primarily Catholic, so we were quick to discover that we were the only Protestants within several miles. This religious diversity has absolutely no bearing on this story; I only mention it to give you a better picture of my old stomping grounds. During my first year of college, I met up with several Christian musicians, and we formed one of the first Christian rock bands in the area, a group we called Bema. Imagine for a moment, if you will, a Christian rock band in the 1970s, in the land of Catholic marble and liturgy! Needless to say, we never received an invitation to play at St. Joseph's, so we spent most of our time gigging in Cincinnati or Covington, Kentucky.

One of our favorite places was a coffeehouse just outside Cincinnati. It was always packed, and they had a pretty decent stage for us to play on. The proprietors of the establishment were a bunch of Jesus freaks who had started a sort of parachurch organization. Many were ex-rockers, ex-druggies, or those who'd been tossed out of their traditional churches for being too radical. We soon became a favorite at the coffeehouse, regulars on the schedule.

The parachurch also had its own Christian rock band, a group called Regal. Their lead guitarist and our rhythm guitarist were former party animals and drug mates; therefore, there was a distinct connection between Bema and the coffeehouse. For those of you who were not around during the charismatic movement of the 1970s, let me explain a few things. First, there were some weird people running around, mostly ex-druggies and church nonconformists. They often bragged about not being involved in organized religion, though many of their parachurch organizations were more controlling than traditional churches; this was certainly the case with those who ran the coffeehouse. They truly believed they owned Regal, too, so they tried to call all the shots for the band. Of course they set up all the gigs and took all the money the band raked in, but they didn't stop there. Every time we played at the coffeehouse, they pressured us to become part of their ministry. Of course there was no way we were going to fall into that trap, as

we all attended our own churches and were quite happy being independent

and calling our own shots. It wasn't long before the pressure to join them

became almost a demand, though, and at that point, Bema decided it was time

to move on. They were simply getting too weird and pushy, so we had to

reject their requests for us to play.

Bema practiced at my house on Thursday evenings. One particular

Thursday, an entourage from the parachurch showed up. I still have no idea

how they knew where or when we practiced, but five raving Pentecostals just

appeared in my parents' basement to advise us that we were outside of God's

will because we had chosen to remain unaffiliated with their quasi-church

organization. Their spokesperson was a women in her 40s, Jean, one of the

founders of the parachurch, and she was backed up snidely by her nephew

Harry. I had known about Jean for a long time because she and her husband

were infamous in the area, having been kicked out of a Methodist church for

attempting to convert all the teenagers into Pentecostals. I don't mean to pick

on my Pentecostal brothers and sisters, but there are two arguments often

used by Pentecostals who are clearly losing a fight: "Thus saith the Lord,"

and, "You just have an issue with being unable to submit to authority." Both

of these were thrown around a lot, to no avail, because we let them know in a

hurry and often that we would never join their group, not under any circumstances. Anyway, as the basement invaders left, Jean handed us a religious tract about the occult and urged us to read it.

"What the heck was that?" we asked each other, completely shocked by the visit. It finally dawned on us that they had decided that Bema simply had to be ensnared, under the power of Satan, since we refused to join up with them. I looked at my bandmates and proudly proclaimed, "Guys, we need to change our name to the Camp Springs Occult Blues Band, in light of this visitation by the prophets Elijah and Deborah!" We laughed for about ten minutes, then decided we preferred to stick with our original name, and Bema we remained.

The story did not end there though. About twenty years later, I ran into Jean at a new church my wife and I began attending. Jean and her husband were members there, and, ironically enough, they became two of the best friends we've ever had, even surrogate grandparents to my kids. Although we never talked about the incident, Jean did say to me one day, "We were pretty much out of control back in the early days of the Jesus movement. We had something, but we didn't know what it was. I'm sure glad the Lord settled us down a bit." It was her best attempt at apology, and it was one I certainly couldn't refuse!

Thrown Off Fountain Square

The 1970s was a strange time. Music was changing, and so were

people. At the start of that decade, there was good, hard rock 'n' roll,

celebrated by longhaired hippies, and it seemed like people actually cared for

each other. Somewhere in the middle of the seventies, though, a big change

hit, and in came disco music and yuppies. The gimme-gimme-gimme

generation had arrived! You've already heard me mention that the first half of

the 1970s was great for bands. Gigs were available everywhere, and almost

any band with even a hint of talent could earn a fairly decent living playing.

Of course that changed big time when disco arrived, but the first half of the

decade was undeniably a great time for musicians.

Even though there were lots of gigs available, bands still had to play

some free shows just for the sake of exposure and advertisement. We had to

be selective about the freebies, though, or we'd just end up wasting all our

stage time trying to get paying gigs, while never actually landing any. A lot of

promoters tried to screw bands over by telling them certain things would look

good on their *RÉSUMÉS* or fibbing with tales of how many bands had "been discovered" via those gigs. We just had to keep our eyes wide open to watch out for those slimy bastards.

One very desirable free gig for bands in Cincinnati was to play on Fountain Square during one of the city's scheduled lunchtime events. The concerts attracted huge crowds, and the best bands in town were usually asked to play. Not only that, but club owners were known to frequent the performances to scope out bands for their clubs, so it was very important not to stink when playing on Fountain Square.

I'm not exactly sure how my band, Stonehenge, landed the Fountain gig, but it was a total surprise to us, since we weren't really the type of band that was usually asked to play there. Most were a bit more laidback, players of top-forty hits. For the most part, Stonehenge was a hard rock band, and we played plenty of Black Sabbath, Blue Oyster Cult, Jimi Hendrix, and other tunes pulled from that genre of music. We were also known to be one of the loudest bands in Cincinnati, so I was more than a little nervous about the lunchtime gig. Really, I feared Stonehenge would fit into Fountain Square about as well as a hooker in church, but we didn't want to squander the rare opportunity. We had a very long song list, with a lot of music to choose from, so that was one thing that would give us a bit of an edge.

There was a technical issue with the Fountain that we were not aware of before we chose our set list though. The stage was a big, metal, clamshell-shaped contraption that acted like a horn in a PA system, amplifying every sound and shooting it right back to the crowd at a deafening volume. The stage was also set up in the inside corner of an L-shaped building, so we had the added benefit of three hard surfaces to project the sound. Of course we chose the loudest stuff, like selections from Sabbath and Hendrix. Basically, we set up a great big stack of amplifiers and PA, and we had a set list of hard-driving tunes in the absolute worst environment possible.

We were about three tunes into the set when the cops rushed onstage and ordered us to turn it down. Usually, in our line of business, the cops showing up meant the party was really taking off, but that was not the case in this scenario. We turned down the volume the best we could and managed about one more tune before they came back, screaming, "Still way too loud!" Our amps were as low as they could go, so all we could do at that point was change the set. I started calling out the most laidback stuff we had, and that brought it down quite a bit, so we managed a few more songs before the boys in blue returned. "If you don't take it down to acceptable levels, we'll cut the power to the stage," they threatened.

We looked at each other and, in what seemed like one voice, blurted, "This is total bullshit!" I then advised the cops, "Look, we've got only one more song to play. Please don't cut the juice just yet." I then looked at the guys and told them, "Crank it up, boys! We'll end with 'Flaming Telepaths!'" If you are not familiar with that particular Blue Oyster Cult hit, you should know it is a very hard, very loud song that ends with several repeats of a line that seemed particularly poignant at the time: "And the joke's on you!" So, with our amps turned back up to eleven where they belonged, we absolutely shook Fountain Square before we left the stage. In the end, I couldn't believe they let us go through with it.

Even though we did not get to play the set we wanted and actually had to shorten our time onstage by quite a lot, we still managed to catch the eye of several club owners and landed some really decent gigs because of that performance. I guess the joke really was on them!

Don't Mess with the Union

Roadies are great, or at least I assume they are, since I've never been at the level where I could hire any. As someone who has always had to handle his own equipment, I can only imagine what it would be like to just ride up to the gate, get out, walk onstage, and start playing, leaving the dirty work to someone else. Even better, maybe I could just give my all onstage, play the last tune, then just get in the car or bus and leave without touching a single amp or mic stand. Someday, right? Wait. Who am I kidding? I'm 55 years old; I haven't had a roadie yet, and I'm pretty sure that ship has sailed. Maybe the aides in the old folks' home will wheel me to the stage and set my rig up for me, but I doubt it. Anyway, being your own roadie isn't all that bad. At least you always know where your stuff is and how it's being treated.

Back in the 1990s, I was a member of a rather large band and vocal group that played Christian contemporary music in the style of the Promise Keepers. I've mentioned this group before, but we were comprised of twenty-two singers and several players, and we were invited to perform at a lot of churches and men's functions. From time to time, we were asked to play some preliminaries for Promise Keepers events in the region, and some of

our vocalists actually participated onstage at the big events, as part of the

choir. We had a lot of equipment, with a full PA, guitar and bass amps,

Hammond organ, Leslie tone cabinet, drums, percussion, and various other

pieces. Loading in and out was not exactly trivial, but with twenty-two-plus

sets of hands, we handled it okay.

As I already mentioned, we typically played smaller venues, such as

churches and school halls. Occasionally, though, we had the opportunity to

play in some really nice places. Case in point: We played at the Nationwide

Arena in Columbus, Ohio, a huge place where many major rock 'n' roll shows

performed. The Promise Keepers were scheduled to hold their regional event

there, and we were asked to a play at a preliminary event the day before, for a

nice-sized crowd. We were pumped, but we had a lot of work to do. Since our

concert would be on the day before the actual Promise Keepers show, we had

to set up our own PA system. Needless to say, we didn't have anywhere near

enough equipment to fill such a large arena, so we had to borrow a lot of

stuff. One of the guys in the band attended a very large church that owned a

lot of gear, so we borrowed subs, power amps, and a large mixing console.

We even commandeered their FOH engineer.

The day of the gig, we loaded up and arrived at the dock with several

vans full of gear and all our performers, excited to play. Before unloading, we

walked in to check out the venue. To say we were amazed would be a complete understatement. Some of the younger guys just stood there looking up at the thousands of seats and the army of people setting up equipment. "Are you sure we're in the right place?" one of them even asked. After assuring everyone that it was the right venue, we headed back out to the dock to bring in our stuff. The schedule was a bit tight, especially since we had to sound check gear we weren't used to. We had about half the first van unloaded, with the gear sitting on the dock floor, when we were stopped dead in our tracks.

It was our first encounter with a union, and we had no idea what was happening. According to the dock workers union, they had a contract with the arena that all equipment was to be unloaded and carried in by them. That wouldn't have been so bad, except that there was no way to tell when they would get around to taking our stuff in. Still, with our hands tied with legal and bureaucratic bullshit, all we could do was sit there looking at each other, watching precious time tick off the clock. Finally, the event organizer had a heart-to-heart with the union steward, only to discover that the union workers were worn out from back-to-back-to-back events. Exhausted and overworked, they didn't much care about our puny batch of gear, so they let us slide. As we say down South, we tore into it like a blind dog in the meat house, as we had a lot of lost time to make up. Fortunately, we had enough PA, albeit just barely, and it turned out to be one of our better gigs. Most of all, we learned a valuable lesson that day: Don't ever mess with the union!

It's Not a Party Until the Police Arrive

As is the case in nearly all professions, musicians love to see their children follow in their footsteps and become even better musicians than they are, although most would prefer that their offspring miss out on all the bad stuff, like the drugs, drinking, hole-in-the wall bars, lack of money, cheating managers, and other such unfortunate issues that occur in the music industry, many of which I've already discussed in these pages. To see your child succeed, to watch them take the music farther and play it much better than you ever could, is a great moment of pride for a parent. I've had the great pleasure of experiencing this twice, with my oldest son and oldest daughter. Both are classically trained and better musicians than I can ever hope to be. My daughter chose not to pursue a career in music, but she certainly has the chops to pick it up and go with it anytime if she chooses to do so. My son, on the other hand, is a musician by profession, and I can proudly say he's doing quite well.

When my two oldest kids were in middle and high school, they both played in the band. My wife and I were active band parents, which meant we chaperoned all the trips, camps, and the like. I must take a moment here to add a bit of commentary: It's highly likely that most of the guys and gals reading this book *didn't* play in the school band. Some of you probably can't even read music and would find such a humdrum thing unnecessary, but I purport that such thinking is bullshit. If you can, put your kids in band. If you happen to be a kid reading this, forgive that curse word a second ago, but haul yourself down to the school office and register for band. Not only will you learn to read music and a great wealth of music theory, but you will also gain discipline, as well as discover how to be a functional part of a group. Plus, those weeklong band trips to Florida, Niagara Falls, Virginia Beach, and other places are huge fringe benefits, memorable times you'll enjoy while everyone else is stuck in class!

Anyway, any active band parent knows it is something of a big deal. Such a role requires a lot of time, dedication, and hard work, but few ever regret it. Many band kids still refer to my wife and me as Mom and Dad because of the relationships we forged with them during our seven great years as band parents. Chaperoning all those trips meant I was the band director's go-fer during the day, and I walked the grounds all night to make sure the guys and girls stayed in their respective cabins. Even though it meant a sleepless week for me, I had a ball, and I can honestly and proudly say no children were conceived on my careful watch. Sometimes in my sleep now, I still hear the drum line playing that same cadence over and over and over again.

During my time as a band parent, there were also several other old rocker types who served as well. This one time, at band camp—my first year there, to be precise—several of us brought guitars so we could do a little pickin' and grinnin' of our own during downtime. We got together at my camper, and it wasn't long before a crowd of kids surrounded us. We were truly shocked by the number of old tunes they knew and requested, so many that we ended up promising to play for a dance on the last night of camp. The old rocker parents and the band directors even joined us in the horn section, and it was such a huge success that it became an annual event. The kids even dubbed us with an honorable name that brought a smile to all our faces: the Old Fogies Band.

Year after year, the Old Fogies got better and better, and the campers always looked forward to the dances. My second-to-last year as chaperone, band camp was held at a religious campground in southeast Ohio. It was a beautiful place, with a huge shelter house that reminded me of an airplane hangar without its walls. Every evening, the full band got together there, after spending the day in sectionals. We also used that building for the Friday night dance. As the band set up, I brought out my PA system, and it wasn't long before we were ready to rock the night away for the kids.

We were about five songs into the first set, and the kids were dancing. As the video cameras rolled, the county sheriff showed up; apparently, a neighbor had called the police to complain about the noise. Man, that felt good, as I hadn't had the police called on me in a long time! One of the other parents yelled, "Hey, man, now it's a real party! The cops are here!" Ah, the lessons we teach our kids! The band director talked to the cop, and after listening to a couple tunes, he decided we weren't that loud, even though we actually were. It worked to our advantage that the sheriff had no problem with a little old-time rock 'n' roll!

Man, Am I in the Wrong Band

Have you ever found yourself playing in a band, only to realize that you don't belong there? It's probably a somewhat common occurrence, although the reasons for feeling that way vary widely. Skill set differences can often present a problem for musicians, because it can be excruciatingly difficult to play in a band if the other musicians are just not up to par or what you are used to. It's easy to find yourself bored when the other guys can't keep up, unless, of course, you're happy to be the so-called star, but that's another story entirely. On the other hand, it's just as difficult to play in a band when everyone else is much better than you, which is usually the case for me! Don't get me wrong: I'm a firm believer in stretching your abilities by playing with more accomplished musicians, but you may find yourself in way over your head. As just one example, I was asked to play bass for a Christmas event with a bunch of extremely accomplished jazz musicians, all of them way out of my league. It was all I could do to keep up, and after the gig, I was emotionally drained. I felt like I had just run a marathon and definitely did not have fun at that gig.

Style preferences, as well as expectations, can be uncomfortable. You may never find musicians whose attitude exactly matches yours, but you should work with people who come close. In other words, you don't necessarily have to sing from the same page, but you should at least be using the same songbook. Sometimes, you'll find that your band is comprised of complete and utter jerks. Whenever that happens to me, I don't feel bad about moving on, no matter how talented the band is. Music is supposed to be fun, and I refuse to let anyone mess that up for me. For a couple years, I played with a church praise band, and the music director was a first-class, certified pain in the posterior muscle. She made life miserable for everyone, but the church liked the clout of having a music director who could boast about having a song or two on the charts. I finally moved on, but it was about a year and eleven months too late.

Just the other day, I received a call from an old friend back in Kentucky, and we talked about a musical situation he faced. That call was actually the catalyst for this story. Troy and I go way back, although we've never had the chance to jam together since we're both bass players. I'll never tell him this, but he was always just a little better than me. I've not heard him recently, but I assume he's still just as good, if not better. We knew each other back in the bar band days and actually started playing Christian music around the same time. Troy has played in a couple Christian rock bands over the years but has spent most of his musical career working with church praise and worship bands.

Recently, a guy Troy works with asked if he would be willing to play bass in a Christian contemporary group, as they would soon be losing their bass player and had gigs scheduled. The band, he said, started out as his church praise band, but they were now playing gigs outside their church, partly because the church would not allow them to play the kind of music they wanted to play. Troy listened in on a gig to check them out and opted to join them. The guys were all decent players, with nice vocal abilities and a nice set list. It didn't take very long for Troy to get up to speed, and before he knew it, he was playing gigs with them. It also didn't take very long for him to notice some odd behavior.

It appeared that the members of the group still considered themselves the church band. At every practice, all conversation was about their church, and they cut practice short on occasion to work on tunes for the next Sunday service. Troy found that some of the guys were quite angry at him when he would not agree to play at special church services, such as Easter and Christmas. He had his own church to attend and simply could not be there for those, but his bandmates didn't seem to see the logic in that. That was not the only sign that they still thought of themselves as the church band though.

A couple of the band members were not what one would consider lead vocalists, yet they insisted on singing lead on several tunes. This is generally okay for a home church audience who knows and loves you, but it's not a good idea when playing an actual gig.

Troy also found himself on the outside looking in when it came to providing input and direction. He suggested several songs and sent MP3 files and chord charts to each of the band members, only to be completely ignored. He even provided a CD of original music for their evaluation; again, no one said a word.

Rather than making a big deal out of the situation, Troy decided to just consider himself a hired gun instead of a band member, to just shut up and play. I could tell by the tone of his voice when he told me this story that it didn't sit well with him. Like me, Troy is a team player who has a great desire to contribute, and working as a hired gun simply does not fill that need. It would be kind of like working for twenty years for a company, only to get fired and rehired as a contractor. Sure, you get to do the same work, but no one wants to hear your input. Troy mentioned that he felt like "the proverbial redheaded stepchild." As such, if he is still with this entirely wrong band by the time you read this story, it wouldn't surprise me if his days with them are numbered.

Auditions

I'll Hire You Guys if My Niece Can Sing Backup

A Freebie from a Good Band

Auditions are always tough for any band, even when they are legitimate, but nothing pisses a band off worse than discovering they've been set up or used to provide free music. Several Cincinnati area bands fell victim to this at the Stagecoach Club in Northern Kentucky. There is little I can say about the owner, other than that I believe any psychological evaluation he'd have to undergo would have to be performed by a proctologist. I can speak with passion about the jerk because my band, Stonehenge, was stupid enough to fall for his scheme.

Stagecoach Club was well known for hosting the top local bands. It was also *the* hangout for the 20-something crowd. The décor was unbelievable, complete with stagecoaches and a blacksmith shop. We found out that the club owner held auditions for bands on Thursday nights, the evenings when his house band was off. We dropped off a demo tape and, within a week, were called in for an audition. We were asked to prepare for an hour-long set of our best music.

When we got there, we discovered that we were the second of three bands to audition that night. The first was pretty good, although the lead guitarist seemed to be stuck in a rut; every lead he played sounded like every other lead he played, but I do have to give him credit for playing a really great rendition of Dan Fogelberg's "As the Raven Flies."

We played our set and really smoked it, though our stuff was a bit harder than the others. In fact, it was probably one of our best sets ever, and we were really on that night. While we were playing, the club owner continued talking with the previous band and didn't seem to be paying much attention to us. Of course we assumed that meant the gig would be given to them. After the set, my lead guitarist and I, who usually handled the business end of things, sat down with the club owner while the third band played. It was quite obvious that he'd had a few too many that night, but in a series of slurs, he did manage to confess that while he really liked his house band, he was ready for a change. He went on to tell us he was willing to give us the gig if we would fire our drummer and hire his nephew instead. We could not believe what we were hearing. I usually hold my temper fairly well, but that night, I told him to kiss my big, red, fat fanny (and, yes, I'm sure I said "fanny").

While we were packing up our stuff, we struck up a conversation with the first band and found out he'd made the exact same offer to them. We later determined that the guy was just using his Thursday night auditions as an opportunity to get free music while his house band was off, and he pulled his hire-my-nephew bit on almost all the bands, hoping somebody would take the bait—or maybe knowing they wouldn't, so he'd just keep getting free performances for his club.

I drove by the site the other day when I was back in town and found that Stagecoach Club is no longer. It has been torn down, and in its place is a lawyer's office. I thought it quite apropos that one den of snakes has been replaced by another.

There Was This Little Sweet Shop…

If you are a full-time musician or know one, you probably understand what it means to live by a calendar: Friday at Starlight Ball Room, filling in with a dance band; Saturday evening playing country at Billy Bob's; Sunday morning at the Presbyterian Church; giving lessons Monday through Wednesday; and spending Thursday in the studio. Musicians have to hustle, and very few land any long-term gigs sufficient for consistently paying the bills. Many musicians, if not most, have to work other jobs to make ends meet. Quite often, players try to stay within the arts to earn additional cash.

Matthias, that fine young musician I've already mentioned a time or two, took on summer gigs doing semiprofessional theater for fun and to pay the bills. Usually, theater gigs require an audition that includes singing, dancing, and delivering a monologue. Depending on the particular play or musical and whether or not the director knows you and your work, some or all of the audition may be waived. The first time Matthias auditioned for a musical, he was advised by the music director that he did not need to prepare a monologue, since he was auditioning for a nonspeaking part; he only had to sing.

The day of the audition, Matthias found himself among a roomful of hopeful performers. Again, depending on the director, the audition may be held behind closed doors, or it could be onstage, in front of all the competition. At this particular audition, Matthias found himself sitting in the theater, watching performer after performer pour their hearts out onstage. For many, that play would be a stepping stone in their careers, just one more show to add to their RÉSUMÉ. For others, it was as good as it got. As you can imagine, the individual performances went from the extremely talented to those who had the director asking, "What the hell were you thinking?" Anyone who has watched preliminary rounds of *American Idol* knows exactly what I'm talking about.

As Matthias sat there watching, he noticed that all the performers had prepared a monologue for their auditions. He didn't have one to deliver, but he wasn't worried about it at first, since he knew the music director and assumed he hadn't been steered wrong. He just assumed that maybe the nonspeaking auditions had not yet started. When his name was finally called, he stepped onstage and delivered a fantastic vocal performance. Knowing he had nailed the song and feeling quite proud of himself, he was ready to leave the stage, but to his horror, he heard the director ask about his monologue.

He politely informed her that he had been advised that a monologue was not necessary but was immediately set straight on the requirements.

Matthias didn't know what to do at that point. He needed the gig, and he'd actually been led to believe the audition was just a formality. All along, he thought the money was in the bank. Now, he had to think quickly, or the gig would be lost, and he'd already spent the take!

There are a couple things you need to know about Matthias before this story continues. First, he has a tremendous ability to store a headful of trivial knowledge. He watches nature and history shows, documentaries, and the like, and he seems to remember countless facts, figures, tidbits, and did-you-knows that will never be of use to anyone. He also watches movies over and over and commits most of the dialogue to memory. I swear, I've heard him quote most of *Monty Python and the Holy Grail* verbatim, as well as the script to *Strange Brew*—both classics, I might add. Armed with this uncanny ability, Matthias was ready to shoot from the hip. Did he launch into something from *The King and I* or some other Broadway show or even a quote from the classics, like all the other performers had done? No, not Matthias! Instead, he opted to recite from the roadie on *Wayne's World 2,* a tale about beating a sweet shop owner to death with his shoe, trying to get jelly beans to bribe Ozzy Osbourne to do a show. Matthias nailed it, right down to the monotone, limey British accent, and a roar of cheers and applause rolled through the theater. The director just sat there holding her side, with tears

running down her cheeks. Needless to say, Matthias got the gig, along with
several more to follow.

Tiny Room

Have you ever played in a really small room, one far too tiny for the tunes you were belting out? I think all musicians have experienced this a time or two. If I can be philosophical for just a moment, I'd like to say I believe these common experiences are what really strengthens the bond between musicians. For instance, two guitar players who've never met before can, within just a few short minutes, be talking and laughing like they've known each other for a lifetime. Why? Because they've shared the same experiences, done the same things, played the same gigs. Maybe they know the same musicians and have the same tools and equipment at their disposal. This is true even if they live 1,000 miles apart and are separated by a generation. You may see this is in other areas, such as with military personnel or police, but I believe the bond between true, down-in-the-trenches musicians is stronger than most.

In my later high school years, I played in a really hard rock 'n' roll band called Journey's End, a name we took from an obituary column in our local paper. We later changed it to Chance, when the better-known Journey came out with their album; we certainly didn't want to be confused with those

losers! As I've already mentioned, my bands often played very hard rock 'n'

roll, including Sabbath, Blue Oyster Cult, and Hendrix tunes. In other words,

we played very loud music, and we were among the loudest. With our stacks

of amps, we could pin an audience to the back wall of any school gymnasium.

We spotted an advertisement in a local newspaper for a club in

northern Cincinnati, The Lancelot Inn, looking for a hard rock band to play

on the weekends. We gave them a call and set up an audition for the middle

of the week. We arrived early enough to catch another band's audition. As it

turned out, they were pretty lame, so we were sure we would wipe the floor

with them. The minute we walked in, though, we knew we just could not play

there. There was a small bar across the right side of the room, but there were

no more than ten or fifteen tables. Truth be told, our basement practice room

was bigger than The Lancelot. Don't get me wrong: It was a very nice club,

well decorated and clean, but, wow, it was small! I couldn't even believe

they'd advertised for a hard rock band. An acoustic Dan Fogelberg/James

Taylor-type group might have done okay there, but the place wasn't fit for

straight-up rock 'n' roll.

We resigned ourselves to the fact that we were not going to take the

gig, but we went through with the audition anyway. We had set the evening

aside and had already carried in our gear, so there was no harm in it. The first

band finished and high-fived each other over their wonderful performance, and we asked them to stick around for our set. Confident that they had blown our doors off, they were happy to stay. We really smoked that performance, and the first band knew their fate. Before we even got through the second tune, they took off, hanging their heads in shame.

Halfway through our set, another band came in for an audition. After we finished, we talked with them and advised them that we were going to pull out of the job. They set up and played, and we stuck around for their entire set. They really were great, and their set list was much more suited to the room. We heard some great music and met some great musicians. We actually kept in touch and shared gig prospects after the fact, so the evening wasn't a total waste.

For the young musicians out there, what is the moral of this story? Make sure you know what you are getting yourself into—and that you can fit in it—before setting up an audition.

The Death Blow: Disco and DJs

I hate disco. I don't mean that I simply dislike it; I seriously, truly despise it, with every fiber of my being. If Dante had written his *Divine Comedy* in the 1970s, I'm sure he would have created a special circle of hell just for the Bee Gees. I hope you are not asking why I hate it so much, because a real musician would never ask such a thing and would understand and completely share my pain. Still, just for the heck of it, let me lay it out for the non-musician. First, the music—a term I use very loosely for disco—has absolutely no substance. It typically consists of nothing more than several variations of one chord, and the lyrics continually repeat the same pointless line, all while the drummer holds the same boring beat, never changing an accent. Of course the same could be said for music in a Pentecostal church, but that's another story entirely. The only musician in a disco band who might possibly have any fun at all would be the bass player or, on rare occasions, the horn section, although, they also usually end up repeating the same riffs over and over again. Your Honor, in defense of this statement, I present to you, as

Exhibit A, KC and the Sunshine Band's "Shake Your Booty," and with that, I rest my case!

Above and beyond my dislike for disco music is the damage the genre did to the music industry itself. Before disco, rock 'n' roll bands ruled the club scene. Gigs were plentiful, even for average players, and a musician could make a fairly decent living playing local bars. When the evil plague of disco descended upon the world, not unlike the locusts upon Egypt in Old Testament times, good rock 'n' roll bands were left in ruin. Why did this great disco plague happen? Perhaps a more appropriate question would be: *How* did this happen? Actually, the death blow occurred in two very swift stages. First was disco music itself. Can someone please explain to me what the heck happened to the intelligence level of the general population in the mid-seventies? How did we go from "Freebird" and "Stairway to Heaven" to "Jive Talkin'," seemingly overnight? I can only assume the abuse of psychedelic drugs during the late sixties and early 1970 finally took their toll on the minds of music listeners. The second blow came from DJs. Back in the fifties, high school dances relied on record players, but that was because there just weren't that many bands around, so vinyl was the best they could do. In the 1970s, DJs became popular simply because of economics, not to mention cheap club owners. Back when I was playing, a four-piece band could earn from $200 to $400 for an evening, so with my dazzling math skills, I can calculate each guy's take to be from $50 to $100. Then, along came the DJ, asking for only $50 to $100 for an entire evening. Guess who landed the gigs.

I would like to share one bad experience I encountered during the disco era. As I've already mentioned in other stories elsewhere in this book, Stonehenge was a straight-up rock 'n' roll band. We performed a variety of stuff from Black Sabbath to the Eagles, but we flat out refused to play disco. Thus, for a time, jobs were very hard to come by, and when we did find them, we had to play in some real holes. Somehow, we managed to get an audition at a very nice club in Cincinnati. The house band fit perfectly into the nine-piece disco/horn mold, but the owner had heard about us and was interested in having us play some special events on the nights when they weren't scheduled. We smoked the audition, and he knew he had an opportunity to hire a really good band, even though we didn't fit the normal demographic. He offered us a private party, advising, "I've got a hunch about you guys." Not only that, but it would be an excellent event to test our appeal on his usual crowd. He indicated that he would call in a day or two with the particulars, and we left feeling all fired up that we'd have the opportunity to play in a large, nice club again, one without chicken wire.

About two days later, the owner called, as promised, but he didn't give us the news we were expecting. His house band found out about our audition and went ape over the gig offer. They waved their contract in the air, pointing to the part that stated that they were to play all the gigs that came along. In reality, he could have told them to take a hike, but I guess he didn't think it was worth the fight. So, once again, we were screwed over by yet another disco-playing, leisure suit-wearing bunch of losers. Now ask me again why I consider disco the scourge of the music world.

Dirty Deeds Done Dirt Cheap

Bands split up and change personnel. It happens. As a matter of fact, the music industry is a bit like a revolving door, with guys constantly moving in and out. It's just a way of life for musicians, something we have to get used to. What's the reason for the constant change? Is there a root cause? Is it unhealthy for the music business? These are all good questions, and there are probably a dozen reasons why someone moves on from a band, either by force or choice. A bandmate may just get pissed for whatever reason and say, "I'm outta here." The band could give one of its members the boot. That is never fun to witness, and I'm happy to say I've not experienced it very often, nor have I ever been kicked to the curb by a band myself. There could be creative differences, but in those cases, the split or departure may be quite amicable.

Sometimes, a good opportunity presents itself for a single band member, something that does not include the whole band. Even if this is emotionally trying for all involved, it is a very good and acceptable reason for someone to leave. I've always believed every musician must look out for him-

or herself and take any and all opportunities that come knocking. I know

many good musicians who've allowed themselves to be held back because of

their loyalty to the band, but music is a cutthroat business, and opportunities

are few and far between. When you have a chance, you have to grab it by the

short-and-curlies. I'm sure your bandmates would, so you're under no

obligation to stay just for their sake. Then again, some musicians are simply

gypsies and seem to have no intention of staying in one band for too long.

Whatever the reason, there is no shame in leaving a band and moving on, but

there can be shame in how you do it.

Personally, I've left a dozen or so bands, but I have always done so

on good terms with all my bandmates. For instance, two years after I left a

band I'd played with for five years, all those guys happily served as

groomsmen in my wedding. Some of my previous bandmates have even

asked me to sit in on gigs when my replacement could not play for one reason

or another. The last thing you want to do is burn bridges, but even more

importantly, you owe a degree of civility to everyone you've shared the stage

with. Being in a band is a sacred bond musicians share, and it should be

honored.

I've heard stories of some horrendously bad band splits, and I want

to share one of the downright dirtiest I've personally been involved with. This

is quite tough for me to talk about, and I debated whether or not to include it, since the main perpetrator is one of my best friends. Of course that may change when he reads this, but I certainly hope it won't.

Pete is not just any ol' drummer; he's a damn fine one, and he takes his music very seriously. He would rather jam than eat, be with his woman, or even drink beer. At the time of this writing, Pete is playing in three bands, yet I'm sure he would still find time to jam with anyone who called him and asked. As we used to say back in high school, man, he's ate up!

Pete got back into music after a twenty-plus-year hiatus, and he jumped back in with an absolute vengeance. I hooked up with him in a classic rock cover band, and we became very fast friends. We played together for almost two years, until I decided to drop out of music for a while to pursue a college degree. I was the lead singer and bass player, and when I left, the band decided to fill my role with a singing guitar player and a bass player. I always knew I was better than any two musicians combined, and that proved it! Of course I say this with my tongue firmly planted in my cheek, because in reality, the band wanted to jump into some guitar-heavy tunes, and my departure gave them the opportunity to do so. With the new guys firmly in place, they started gigging again, but after about six months, their new bass player decided to move on. Once again, they found themselves looking for a replacement. They placed an ad in the classifieds and were soon contacted by a fairly decent player, so they set up an audition. That was precisely when things got weird.

After the audition, the bass player pulled Pete and the singer/guitarist aside and informed him that he also played in another band that could use a better drummer, as well as an additional guitar player with vocal abilities. He asked if they were interested. "Hell yes!" they both said and agreed to jam with the band and give it a try. After the initial jam session, that band kicked their drummer out and invited Pete and the guitar player to join. It is difficult to even imagine how the two guys in the original band felt, because they were completely blindsided and were understandably pissed beyond imagination. As a friend of Pete's and of the guys from the original band, I felt like I was caught in the middle, especially since I talked frequently with all of them. I know for a fact that the guys in the original band have never completely forgiven Pete and the guitar player. They did get a bit of revenge, though, because the new band turned out to be a nightmare for Pete.

The band leader was a real prick, and Pete could not satisfy his musical demands, no matter what he did or how hard he tried. That guy rode poor Pete like a two-dollar whore! One night while they were practicing at Pete's house, Pete got so pissed at the leader's constant belittlement of his playing that he kicked the band out and told them never to return. "Take your crap and get out of my house!" he screamed. "I don't have to take this from you!" It took Pete almost a year to hook up with another band and play out again, but I think he learned a valuable lesson about not screwing over his bandmates, even if his career takes him in another direction.

Three Days of Work Outta Me for Nothing

I don't see why anyone would plan to enter the insane world of politics, but if you are, I highly suggest that you prepare for the position by first taking a job in large church. I can almost guarantee that you will tread more brutal waters there than in any public office. One would think that since church folk are presumably doing the Lord's work and are commanded to be Christ-like, working among the local flock would be like heaven on Earth, but it can be a most grueling task indeed. Don't get me wrong: Church work does have its rewards, especially for those who have a calling for it, but I suggest you do a real gut check before pursuing a career in the church. As an active member of a church currently and a former paid staff member, it is very difficult for me to share this story. It feels as if I'm ratting out a good friend or relative, but I can't deny that some heinous stuff goes on in churches, so it is only fair that I share these stories as well.

I retired from a very good job in corporate America at the ripe old age of 45. The company was in the midst of some moderate downsizing and offered some very nice early retirement packages. One was called the Rule of

70: Years of service plus age equaling or greater than 70 enabled one to retire. I hit that mark by two months, but I was, in fact, the youngest to ever retire from the company. Part of my package included money to cover the cost of training for another career. I checked with my financial guy and found that I had enough in my retirement account that I could actually retire and sit on the front porch in a rocking chair, as long as I died by the age of 60. Since I've always hoped to live a little beyond that, I thought I should take advantage of the training, so I did one of the most enjoyable and probably smartest things in my life and enrolled in sound engineering school.

The school I chose was set up something like a boot camp. I lived there for eight weeks, recording and mixing bands, along with spending tons of time in class, nearly 'round the clock. Man, did I learn a bunch, and I had a fantastic time doing it!

After graduating at the top of the class, I went in search of a job as a technical director in a church. I also looked into other fields, but my main objective was to relocate and hopefully land a dream job in a medium to large church. After months of searching and an occasional interview, I came across what looked like a fabulous opportunity at a very large, growing church in Indiana. It was definitely a relocation opportunity, but it was also only a couple hours from my current home, which would allow me to visit my family often. I submitted my *RÉSUMÉ* and received a call from the worship pastor, the relatively young son of the senior pastor. I did a little research and found out that potential employer was loaded with cash, as the church was located in a very affluent community, and they had money to spend. Also, their huge staff included a worship leader from a very well-known Christian band. I exchanged many emails and phone calls with the worship pastor; in hindsight, I realized some of his questions should have roused my suspicions, but they didn't at the time.

For example, once it was determined they were interested in me visiting for an interview, he requested that I send a photo of myself. I knew it is illegal to ask for a photo before an interview, so it did set off alarms in my head, but I ignored that and complied. It became obvious during the interview why such a request was made. When I asked the senior pastor about diversity, he squirmed in his seat and provided a well-rehearsed and lame but safe answer. That was reinforced when I observed the lily-white congregation at all three services.

Let me describe the actual interview and visit to the church, which took three full days. Of course they wanted me to have a one-on-one talk with nearly every staff member, as well as design the stage and set the lights for the weekend service, as well as run sound checks for all three services. Again, alarms went off in my head, but once again, I ignored the red flags and agreed. I advised them that my wife and young daughter would be traveling with me so she could check out the town and housing, so the third neglected alarm was that no arrangements were made for my wife to tour the area, as they promised. The fourth started blaring when I discovered that even though the church was rolling in cash, they would only put us up in the cheapest hotel in town. The carpets in that hellhole were soaked, and they squished under our feet when we walked in. Honest to God, we couldn't even put our things on the floor, for fear of water damage. There were people cooking on cheap little throwaway grills in the parking lot just so they wouldn't have to incur restaurant expenses.

In spite of those frustrations, the interview process seemed to go pretty well, although it got a bit boring by the time I got through my sit-down with the ninth or tenth pastor of something or other. The final interview was with the senior pastor, who just so happened to be the exact same age as me. We actually seemed to relate to one another quite well, until the diversity question came up. Even then, I think he believed he'd properly glossed over it.

With interviews complete, it was time to design the stage, my mission, if I chose to accept it. That mission impossible should have sounded the fifth alarm and should have sent me running, but it didn't. I was supposed to design a stage, with no previous knowledge of the sermon subject, around a beach theme. I found various beach paraphernalia among their props, including a boat sail, which was oddly cool to see in a church storage room. I spent two whole days stretching the sail and climbing around the very narrow system of catwalks to set lights. Positioning those lights was really an absolute pain and quite dangerous, considering where some of the cans were placed. I actually climbed down out of the extremely high ceiling just ten minutes prior to sound check and took my place behind the console, dirty and sweaty, since I didn't even have a chance to shower and change. I was entirely unfamiliar with their console, of course, but I still managed to get everything sounding absolutely fantastic. If I can brag a bit, I do have a great ear for that sort of thing, so the mission wasn't all that impossible for me after all.

The first service started immediately after the sound check, and I hoped the smelly guy behind the console would not offend any church members or that my disheveled appearance and rather noxious odor would not have a negative impact on the interview process.

I can honestly say that by the time I made it through the first service, I had already decided I would not take the job even if it was offered to me, which it ultimately wasn't. It turned out okay, though, because just a few days later, I was offered the job I currently hold, at more than twice what that wealthy church was offering. I know I am treated a whole lot better where I am, with a lot less politics to deal with. As for the church where I interviewed, at least they got a nice stage setup, great sound for three services, and three days of work, and it only cost them around sixty bucks for a two-night stay in a crappy hotel and a modest lunch after the final service.

Dogged by My Own School

Rock 'n' roll musicians and high school principals just don't mix. This was especially true back in the early 1970s, when most principals were of the older generation and just didn't get the rock 'n' roll crowd. In my case, it didn't help that my principal was the king of jerks. I know what you're thinking: "Hey, buddy, quit with the woe-is-me! Everybody's principal was a jerk. It's sort of a job requirement." That may be true, but I can guarantee that no one was practiced more, enjoyed it more, or accomplished more in the fine art of butthole-ness than Mr. Woods. If there was a class called Creep 101, I'm sure he got straight-A's in it and always asked for extra credit work. Rumor had it that he had framed portraits of his favorite proctologist hanging on the wall in his office. I know I'm making a bold statement here about how bad the guy was, but the following examples of his behavior will confirm my assessment of the guy.

Along with just being downright mean, Mr. Woods also had three major hang-ups, things he could not stand: smoking, long hair, and facial hair. As for smoking, he always hid out near the usual spots just before lunch and between classes, in the hopes of catching someone in the act of lighting up. If he was in a rare good mood, the juvenile smokers would suffer only detention. Most of the time, though, it resulted in a three-day suspension. I remember standing outside a doorway with a cigarette in my hand when Mr. Woods seemed to materialize out of thin air. I managed to cup the cigarette in my palm and place my hand in my pocket, but I damn near caught my pants on fire waiting for him to shut up and move along.

His second major issue was long hair. Our school had a dress code that required boys' hair to be shorter than the collar, and it absolutely could not hang below the ears. Explain to me how a seventies musician was supposed to abide by that rule! Guys in bands actually wore wigs with their hair tucked up under them in order to comply with the code. One guy I knew was busted by Woods for long hair, and after the ration of crap Woods heaped upon him, he actually went home and got a buzz cut. The next day, Principal Woods jumped him again, claiming he only buzzed his hair to get attention. My friend was so pissed that he shaved his entire melon that night, just out of spite, and of course Woods then suspended him for insubordination.

Another thing Mr. Woods simply could not abide was facial hair of any sort. He made rounds through all the homerooms every morning, on the prowl for dress code violations. I had been in a car accident and damn near ripped my upper lip off, so I had received several stitches. Needless to say, I could not shave. He stepped into my homeroom and ripped me a new one in front of everyone about my mustache, which I thought actually looked really great and hid the doctor's needlework well. I tried to tell him about the car wreck, to explain why I was breaking his strict laws, but he wouldn't have it. Instead, he told my homeroom teacher that if I came in the next day with the mustache, I was to be sent to the office.

When I returned to class the next day and still had not encountered a razor, I was promptly kicked out of class. When I got to Woods's office, he was in a conference with the superintendent, and I could not believe how sickly sweet he was to me, putting on a show for his superior. It was my good luck, though, because I went the rest of the year without shaving and had a real nice 'stache by prom time!

Now that you understand Woods's personality or lack thereof, I'll continue with my discussion of his disdain for musicians. Please forgive me if I'm wrong, but isn't being a principal all about education? Good educators are aware that students are watching their every move and, hopefully, learning good things from observing that behavior. Woods, however, failed miserably when it came to the watch-me-and-learn kind of education.

I already mentioned that as a student, I played in a band called Journey's End. It was a pleasure to play with that great bunch of musicians, and we all attended the same school. I was the last to graduate, quit, or be kicked out, but that's another story. We were quite popular with the school clubs that sponsored dances, and we had auditioned for an upcoming dance and been given the job. We followed the same process we always did for school gigs, agreeing on a price and setting the date. About two days before the gig, I heard a few rumors that the dance had been canceled, but the sponsors hadn't said anything to us about it. Since I wasn't sure if it was just idle gossip or not, I headed to the office to get the scoop. I asked Principal Woods if the dance had been canceled, and he matter-of-factly advised, "Yes, it's been canceled for weeks." I was understandably pissed and asked why the band was not informed, since it was how we made a living. When I explained that we might have missed out on another gig because we had no idea that one was canceled, Woods simply replied, "Well, did you sign a contract with the club?" He knew the answer to that already, since clubs were not authorized to sign contracts with anyone. When I didn't bother to answer, he just looked at me with a crap-eating grin on his face, as if to say, *"Ha! I just got one over on a bunch of longhaired, hippie musicians!"* Had he been a real educator, he would have worked with the club to show them how important it was to honor their commitments and also the importance of follow-up. Instead, he chose to show his colossal jerkism once again.

In the end, Mr. Woods was finally removed from office. Of course the school system made it look like a promotion, but in reality, they just shifted him into a nothing job just to get him away from people.

Managers

Dude, Where's Our Money?

Damn Near Made It but Got Screwed Over by a Has-Been

I have to be real careful about how I write this story, since it makes reference to several very well-known folks. As I stated at the outset, I will take some poetic license to protect the innocent as well as the guilty, in order to keep myself from being involved in a lawsuit, though I want it to be clear that I have no intention of writing gossip columns about the stars. It's really a story about a very talented local who had a good shot at making it but was instead crapped on by a has-been.

Rudy Taylor was a guitar player in one of my old bands, as well as one of the best friends I ever had. He was absolutely fabulous on the guitar, and back in the day, he was the real talent in my band. Even though I was the front man and a damn fine lead singer, if I do say so myself, I still think of Rudy as our superstar. Now, before we carry on with this story, for those of you who are just starting out, it is BigBassMan editorial time again.

Opportunities in the music business do not always present themselves to bands; very often, they are only offered to individual members.

You may feel like a heel leaving your buds behind, as we discussed in a previous chapter, but if someone dangles a carrot in front of you, you'd be a fool not to take it. In fact, count yourself lucky for the chance, because I can almost guarantee you will not get a second one. It might piss your friends off, but surely they'd jump at a chance themselves if one came their way. Now that the sermon is over, we can get back to our story.

Rudy had a distant cousin who sang backup for a well-known country artist in Nashville. That country singer was definitely on the downside of his career, so it was safe to say that staying with him was not going to lead anywhere. Rudy's cousin, Carrie Sue Taylor, was a very fine singer and decided to make a run at a solo career. She signed with her boss's record label and began working on an album. Carrie Sue had some great songs, and the label set her up with the very best studio musicians to record the music. It was not very long before she had a very good album and was ready to go on the road to promote it. She started putting her band together and lined up some of the best musicians in Nashville, and she gave her cousin Rudy a call to request that he step in as her guitar player. Even though it was a tremendous honor, as well as a once-in-a-lifetime opportunity, Rudy almost passed it up for two reasons. First, he didn't want to leave the band. Second, he was a rock 'n' roller, and country just didn't appeal to him all that much. After smacking him in the face with a chair, I told him to get his butt to

Nashville before the sun went down. After some soul-searching, he finally called Carrie Sue and told her he would take the gig.

Within a week, Rudy was in Music City to practice with the band. He gave me a call and told me he had never felt so outclassed in all his life. Carrie Sue's drummer was the current drummer at the big music show in Nashville, which I don't think I need to name. The bass player was the road player for another popular Nashville female singer, who was too busy making movies to go on tour at that time. The piano player was also the band leader and had served as the longtime pianist for a Nashville icon, but that superstar was currently tied up in one of his many rehabs or jail visits. There were a fiddler and steel guitarist, but I'm not sure if they were permanently connected to anyone of notoriety. Even though Rudy had to struggle to keep up, within a few practices, the band was ready for the road.

Of course an interesting thing happened on the way to the road. It turned out that the county singer Carrie Sue had backed up for years was not really happy when she left him. As a matter of fact, he was mad as hell. Personally, I think he was jealous and was just out for revenge, determined to shut her down. He contacted some of his cronies at the record label and managed to convince them to delay the release of her album. Without a record to promote, there was no reason to tour, so Carrie Sue sadly began canceling shows. All the while, Rudy was morphing into the proverbial starving artist, since he wasn't playing anywhere else. As it became evident that the album would not be released, Carrie Sue decided to switch labels, and

that dragged her into a nasty legal battle. She had no choice but to send all the

musicians home with her sincere apologies, advising them that she had no

idea when the mess would be straightened out.

It was such a shame that such a great artist, the one Carrie Sue used

to back up, felt compelled to shut down two promising careers. He could

have been a hero and helped her, an up-and-comer, as well as possibly even

breathed some life back into his own career, but instead, he decided to play

the spoiler. What an ass!

Fined for Not Smiling, Drinking, Being Late, and Being out of Uniform

Jack Snow is not only one of the best drummers I've ever heard, but he is also, without a doubt, the finest human being on the planet. Jack spent his Christmas Eves delivering presents to underprivileged kids, many of which he paid for out of his pocket. My favorite Jack Snow story was the time when a guy from a poor, inner-city church asked him where he could get a very good price on a set of drums. Jack told him the name of a music store and the person to speak with there. He then called the store and told his friend, the store owner, to only charge the guy $100 for whatever set he chose, and he would pay the difference. It was a good deed the church never even found out about, but what a guy!

Jack has been in the local music business for a very long time and probably has enough stories to fill a book of his own, but he was gracious enough to share several of them with me. One of my favorites is about Showtime, his extremely polished and professional top-forty show band. They were a very large group, complete with female backups and their own horn section. It isn't easy to explain what I mean by "polished." Yes, they were very tight musically, almost too tight—so much that at times, it was hard to tell if they were actually playing or just blaring a recording. Their look was nothing short of amazing, with the girls in frills and lace and the guys in leisure suits. They had several colors of suits and changed often, sometimes right in the middle of their shows. Even all that doesn't adequately explain the degree of "polished" I'm talking about, so let me attempt to describe it another way.

The trumpet player of Showtime was also the manager. In his eyes, it was really all about the money, and the only way to make that money was to put forward the best product possible. For that reason, there were lots of rules, very strict ones that no one dared to break or even bend. Some were logical: For instance, band members were forbidden from drinking onstage, getting the least bit drunk during a performance, or being out of uniform. Others, though, were definitely on the crazy side. He placed spotters in the crowd to watch every member of the band at all times and noted whether or not they smiled as they played, and heaven help those who were caught chewing gum! The penalties for these infractions varied, but they usually included fines. Since he was the manager and collected the money, those fines were easily deducted right out of the band members' paychecks. Of course the most severe penalty was firing, and it was not unusual for someone to be let go mid-set. The female backups seemed to be a favorite target for pink slips, so the band went through several.

Jack and the manager had grown up together and were best friends, so of course the manager designated Jack as the official hatchet man. That's right: Mr. Salt of the Earth had to give those folks the bad news. Jack took it so hard that many times, in a serious role reversal, the person being fired had to console him! Again, what a guy!

On a side note, I find it amazing yet somehow apropos that the manager went on to be the principal of a Catholic grade school, as if nuns whacking their rulers across kids' knuckles wasn't enough!

Just a Beanbag Chair and a Mattress

You may have noticed that I speak of the 1970s with great affection. I guess we all look back at our late teens and early 20s as the good ol' days, and I'm no different. I consider my generation the last of the hippies and basically the end of good music as we knew it, at least for the next twenty-five years. We had a lot going for us back then, including great music and bands, as well as many awesome venues in which to hear and play live music. I know I keep harping on this subject, but disco music and DJs really did put some serious hurt on the live music scene. In the early to mid-70s, gigs were plentiful, and almost every bar or club offered live performances. High schools and fraternities hosted dances every weekend, and even firehouses got in on that once in a while. As the gigs began to dry up in the latter half of the decade, bands had to work harder for every gig. They also found themselves listening to and trusting some fairly shady individuals while they searched for that work. Out of desperation, my band, Stonehenge, found itself mixed up with one of these guys.

During that period of slow gigs, bands found themselves playing a lot of freebies for the sake of promotion and exposure. Even bands that were used to steady paychecks had to play for nothing from time to time, just to ensure they wouldn't be forgotten. My band played one such gig that many bands in the Cincinnati area actually fought hard to get, even though it was a freebie. I already told you about our gig at Fountain Square, but this story actually deals with someone we met after that gig.

As I previously explained, the Fountain Square concerts were held in the middle of the week, during lunch hour, so a nice-sized crowd was almost guaranteed. A real mix of people hung out there. Of course there were the suits and ties, the business people who stepped out of their offices and cubicles for some fresh air and a bite to eat, but there were also out-of-town shoppers. Sprinkled amongst these were the usual drunks, druggies, and bums, along with a few remnants of the hippie generation. Fountain Square also seemed to attract street preachers, politicians, and protestors, simply because there was always a crowd to hear their rants. On days when bands played, many club and bar owners stopped by to scout out the local talent, and that was our main motivation for wanting to land those gigs so badly. We could also count on meeting several wannabe managers, ready to drop their well-rehearsed line of bullshit on any unsuspecting musicians; they kind of reminded us of those two guys on *In Living Color*, who always ended up at the Hollywood parties, posing as big-time agents, handing out someone else's business cards with their names scribbled on it, with the lame excuse that they had run out of their own. It wasn't uncommon to meet that type at Fountain Square, but to be quite honest, a band could run into them at just about any gig. They were chronic namedroppers who supposedly hung out with all the local club owners and claimed to set up gigs galore.

At our Fountain Square gig, we met a guy who seemed a bit different. At first, I thought he was one of those slick, wannabe managers, but he seemed a bit less full of himself, a little more reserved. Instead of bragging that he could land us a ton of gigs, he casually wrote down the names and numbers of several club owners and told us to give them a call. Of course our guitar player took his number and called him several times to thank him for the leads and also to get additional contacts. He invited us over to his apartment one evening, so we piled into the van to make the trip. He lived right next to the university, in the party part of town, but this begs a bit of an explanation before I move on.

Yes, we were musicians, and we were used to partiers. Of course we'd all smoked pot a time or two, and on occasion, we even partook in a little speed, but we had never been around bona fide, strung-out, tracks-in-their-veins heroin users until that night. We walked into the two-room apartment, just a kitchen and a space that functioned as both a living room and bedroom. The kitchen wasn't furnished at all, and the other area was only occupied by a beanbag chair, a mattress on the floor, and a small TV and stereo, also on the floor. Strewn haphazardly across that beanbag chair was the alleged girlfriend.

At that point, this Kentucky boy began to really freak out. Sure, I've done a lot of drinking, often in excess, and I've smoked pot and even popped a few pills I shouldn't have, but I had never seen anyone actually shoot up heroin before. The broad was as skinny as a rail and as white as a sheet, and there was no doubt she was an addict who'd just finished shooting up.

We all looked at each other in total amazement and, just to be polite, accepted a beer, then sat on the floor to discuss possible gigs, ever keeping one eye on the drugged-out girlfriend. Never in my life had I so badly wanted to be elsewhere, and I could tell my bandmates felt the same. After sticking around for what we deemed an appropriate amount of time for good manners' sake, we booked out of there, and we made sure to lose that guy's phone number in the process.

Equipment

Hey, Man, Your Amp Is on Fire!

The Music Is Free, and You're Just Paying Us To Haul This Crap in and out

At times in my life, I would have given my left hangy-down thing—shall we say—for a few good roadies. That was especially true when my band played at the Cold Springs, Kentucky firehouse. To understand my angst, you really need to conjure up a mental picture of the architecture.

The firehouse had a party hall on the second floor, right above the garage where the firetrucks were stashed. In reality, though, the second floor was more like the third or fourth floor, because the first-floor ceiling was extremely high to accommodate the heavy equipment parked inside. There was no elevator, and the only access was really via two steel fire escapes, one on the north side of the building and the other on the south side. To make matters worse, the metal stairs were fairly narrow. Talk about one great big pain in the backside! It was hard enough to even climb the stairs with nothing in our hands, let alone while lugging heavy music equipment up them.

In the 1970s, amps and PA cabinets were far bulkier and heavier than they are today, and keyboards were not as compact as modern ones. It was probably a hilarious sight to see bands hauling those overgrown Hammond

organs up those fire escapes. I had always assumed bands of that era didn't

have keyboard players because good ones were hard to find, but looking back,

I am beginning to think it is just because they didn't want the added burden

of carrying keyboarding gear in and out. Most keyboard players require some

type of electronic piano, maybe a synthesizer, as well as an amp to drive it.

Also, be assured that no respectable keyboardist would be caught dead

without a Hammond organ and at least one Leslie tone cabinet. If you hired a

keyboard player, you had to have a strong back and a weak mind, or else you

just really wanted to play "A Whiter Shade of Pale!" Even bands without

keyboardists cringed at the thought of playing at that Kentucky firehouse. I

knew a few who turned the gigs down simply because they did not want the

hassle of loading in and out.

More often than not, the party room was rented out for wedding

receptions, so the issue was not just one for bands to contend with. Caterers

hated bringing in meals, and bakers were not fond of toting tall, tiered

wedding cakes up those precarious steps. Occasionally, dances and private

parties were held there, but no matter what the event was, it was a sure thing

that the alcohol would flow freely, which only made those steps even more

interesting. Many-a-drunken groomsman ended up flat on his face at the

bottom of those metal steps. In fact, I'm quite surprised no lawsuits were filed, though back in the 1970s, when we all understood that coffee is

supposed to be hot, folks weren't as sue-happy as they are today.

In spite of all our fussing about hauling in and setting up, there was

even more daunting a task before us when it came to striking the stage and

carrying all that crap out, the glamorous part of rock 'n' roll no one ever hears

about. We hauled all our stuff up those horrible stairs, set it up, and played

for several hours. Then, after way too many beers, we had to tear it down,

pack it up, and haul it out, back down three flights of wet, slippery, steel

stairs, tipsy as we were. Ah, the rock 'n' roll life!

I already mentioned giving my left hangy-down for a few roadies, but

I damn near lost it on those freaking stairs! Thank God they eventually tore

down that building and erected a new one, in which they wisely placed the

party room in the basement, complete with walkout access. Now, no jock

straps are necessary for a firehouse gig!

Twenty-Seven Eight-by-Ten Glossies

This story could easily top the no-way-that-happened category, but I assure you that it actually occurred and is not just a recap of some old *Twilight Zone* episode. Our Stonehenge, if I do say so myself, was a very popular hard rock band in the Cincinnati area during the early to mid-seventies, and we actually prided ourselves on how much equipment we owned, some of it fairly good stuff. Finding a practice facility was always a challenge, so we usually resorted to determining which of our parents was in a generous mood, then took up residence there. As soon as we wore out our welcome, we moved on to the next household, placing our trust in those parents' good graces. During one of our cycles, a most inconvenient thing happened at the home of our drummer, Charlie.

Of course the theft of most of our equipment isn't the unique part of this story, because this sort of thing happens to bands all the time. The exciting part of this macabre tale is how it was stolen and how we recovered it.

Before jumping into the story, though, I need to describe one of the main characters, Helen, our drummer's mother. She was a really sweet lady, albeit a bit naïve, gullible, and extremely trusting to a fault. I don't mean any disrespect here, but Helen reminded me of Edith Bunker. Now that I think about it, her husband was a bit like Archie, but there's no reason to get into that right now.

As I said, we were at Charlie's place during a very good period as far as gigs went. We were booked almost every weekend, and someone from the band was always hauling something in or out of the basement. One particular early afternoon, a couple guys appeared at the front door, and Helen greeted them in her usual cheerful way. They explained that they had purchased an amp and speaker cabinet from our guitar player, Rudy, and that they were there to pick it up. They mentioned the names of all the guys in the band, and they also offered some chummy information, as if we had all been buds forever. Being the trusting individual Helen was, she smiled and said, "Well, all that stuff is in the basement, and I'm sure your amp is there. Feel free to just go on down and get it."

Of course no one in the band knew those guys, and Rudy hadn't sold an amp to anyone. To this day, we still don't know how they knew where we were practicing. To say the least, they cleaned us out of amps and PA gear. As a matter of fact, we considered ourselves lucky that all our guitars had gone home safely with their respective players, or they would likely have been picked up on the five-finger discount too.

I could not believe it when Charlie called me to tell me about the theft that night. The police launched an investigation and questioned all the neighbors to see if anyone had seen or recognized the thieves. The next-door neighbor remembered seeing them drive off, because she noticed that their car had a parking sticker for a high school in the next county, the same school she'd graduated from. The police took Helen to the high school, and she reviewed several years' worth of yearbooks. She recognized the two guys' photos, and the police promptly hauled them in for questioning. It didn't take long for them to start singing, and they told the cops where they'd stashed our equipment. As it turned out, they were members of a band who had a steady gig at a local Holiday Inn, and our equipment was all set up right there on that stage, every last bit of it that they'd pilfered. I have no idea what they were using before acquiring our stuff, but they must have liked ours better.

We were quite excited to get our gear back, since we had a gig to play that weekend, but we were disgruntled to find out that it wasn't going to happen as planned. At that point, the local Highland Hills Police Department was hit with the Officer Obie syndrome; anyone familiar with Arlo Guthrie's "Alice's Restaurant" will know exactly what I mean. Since that grand theft audio was the biggest crime to ever hit the town, the police wanted to get everything right. Instead of the typical twenty-seven eight-by-ten glossies of

Officer Obie fame, the Highland Hills Police Department decided they

needed to keep all our equipment at the police station as evidence, until the

trial. That joke of a police station was nothing more than two rooms,

consisting of a small reception area and the chief's modest-sized office. If we

weren't so upset about not having our equipment, it might have been funny,

but we really didn't find it humorous at all. Crammed in that small room were

our two stacks of PA cabinets, mixing console, huge bass cabinet, two guitar

cabinets, and assorted mic stands and cables. The poor desk sergeant looked

like dock security at a Jimi Hendrix concert.

We immediately went into scramble mode, attempting to put

together enough gear for our upcoming shows. Luckily, we were tight with

several other bands, and they were willing to share some of their spare

equipment, so we survived until the police let our equipment out of custody.

Fortunately, they didn't actually hold our gear until the trial, because they

soon discovered they just could not function without any office space.

Instead, they resorted to taking *"TWENTY-SEVEN* eight-by-ten *COLOR*

GLOSSY PICTURES WITH CIRCLES AND ARROWS AND A..." If you

don't understand that, I suggest that you download "Alice's Restaurant" and

listen to the part about Officer Obie. When you do, it will all become crystal

clear!

Phone Sex in Church

Phone sex in church? Surely I've got your attention now! As a matter of fact, it wouldn't surprise me if you took one look at my Table of Contents and flipped straight to "House Band in a Whorehouse," then "Hillbillies Love It in the Hay," then here. Admit it! You oughtta be ashamed of yourself.

Anyway, this story makes me smile or even laugh out loud every time I think about it. Let me set the scene for you: I was attending a fairly small church, and they were quite progressive when it came to the style of music they enjoyed. As a matter of fact, the church band was also my R&B/old rock 'n' roll band that gigged on weekends. I know some of you old-line Baptists might have a stroke over that, but nothing that came out of those speakers ever hurt anyone, and of course the quality of music was about as good as it gets. The church also did a lot in the way of drama, and a good number of their members had remarkable theatrical talent. The youth director was a theater major in college and really knew his stuff, so some of the productions were simply amazing, especially considering that there were only 200 members. Of course by now, you might be asking, "Dude, what does any of this have to do with phone sex in a church?" Just hold your horses, because I'm getting there, you pervert!

As I said, the church was very involved with theater, and since they had a great pool of musical talent to boot, it only made sense that many of the performances were musicals. One was written and directed by the youth director, a modern-day telling of *The Passion of the Christ*. The play was filled with music, much of which I recorded beforehand. One very touching scene that left the audience speechless took place just after the crucifixion, when Christ was placed in a body bag and carried down the aisle and out the back door. Even now, I am overcome with chills as I remember it.

Many had to be involved to pull off such a remarkable production. In fact, there were so many adults that the director had to recruit young stagehands, mostly middle school boys. He rounded up five or six to help with props, change sets between scenes, direct actors on and off the stage, and be his runners. They all did a wonderful job, and it was a real thrill for the kids. They felt very important, because they were, but what made them feel even more important was that they each got to wear a wireless headset that allowed them to communicate with each other, as well as with the director. Unfortunately, those headsets also became the source of a problem. Many such walkie-talkie devices operate at a frequency range in the same spectrum occupied by the signals of cordless telephones. Saying that alone, I am sure you can imagine where this story is headed, but hang with me for just a bit, so I can take you to the climax.

Thursday evening, a dress rehearsal was scheduled, and everyone was onsite and ready to go. The boys all received their headsets and had fun playing with them. They had too much fun, as a matter of fact, and the director had to get on them a time or two, reminding them that the headsets were not toys and were only for official use. They settled down, and rehearsal went very well until it happened: A sexy female voice came across the headsets, saying things that would have made a sailor blush. Apparently, a young lady in one of the houses just across the street from the church was sitting in her bathtub, talking on her cordless phone to her boyfriend, describing, in great detail, exactly what she was doing during her soak and what she planned to do to her lover when he got there. Let me tell you, she sure knew what went where and why, and she had a very vivid imagination about how to accomplish it! The boys' eyes went wide, and giggles broke out all over the church. The director, who also heard the stray transmission, went ghostly white and lost his ability to speak for what seemed like an eternity. When his wits finally returned, he screamed into the mic in a total panic, "Get those headsets off now! I mean right now…and bring them to me!" Of course the boys took their good, sweet time, but they eventually complied. He collected the headsets and sat there flustered for a while, but he somehow managed to collect himself, and rehearsal continued without the headsets.

For the next two evenings, during the actual shows, he allowed the units to be used again but always with a stern warning: "If that, uh, lady-in-waiting returns, you boys turn those off!" Much to the chagrin of the pre-pubescent stagehands, she did not return to the airwaves, but for weeks after that sultry incident, every time I went to church, I saw those boys giggling amongst themselves on the steps, pointing at the house across the street, obviously wondering if that naked lady was still sitting in her tub.

You Can't Even Trust the Bible Belt

Out of everything I've written in this book, this is the toughest story, because on the very morning that I penned it, I heard about the passing of its main character, Rudy. I wrote several stories about him, and this one was already in my plans, but after his wife called me this morning, I decided it had to be included, perhaps as a bit of therapy for my aching heart. I'm sure the vast majority of you have never heard of Rudy, except what you've read in previous pages, but I can assure you that the world just lost one of the best guitar players ever to grace the stage of any honky-tonk bar. Personally, I just lost one of the best friends I've ever known.

Before meeting Rudy, I was just a geeky kid who could sing and play a little bass. In fact, Rudy was almost singlehandedly responsible for showing me the real side of music and jolting me from geek to front man. Even then, I knew and always will know who the real talent in that band was. I can still hear him affectionately calling me Wildman, just as he always did. Dude, I love and miss you!

Rudy always had the chops to make it big, so I assumed he would leave the band anytime. As it turned out, I took off before he did, though it certainly wasn't because I had made it in the music business. Even after my departure from the band, we remained the best of friends, and he was even the best man in my wedding. As I always knew would be the case, Rudy was eventually noticed by some talent in Nashville and received a call to tour with a budding country star. Even though he was a rock 'n' roll guitarist at the time, he had the ability to play country lead like no one else; of course he did, considering that all of us had country backgrounds and even played a few country gigs to make ends meet during the horrid disco days, when a rock 'n' roll gig couldn't be bought. Rudy could play Hendrix and Black Sabbath note for note, so I was sure playing Merle Haggard wouldn't be much of a challenge for him.

Rudy loaded his gear into the van and headed south to what all of us knew would be a great career. Being a musician, you can surely sympathize with the fact that he had little money, so his first night in Nashville was spent in a cheap motel. He didn't know the area that well, and he was somewhat young and naïve, so he didn't exactly choose the best part of town. He wasn't too worried about it, though, considering that Nashville was basically the buckle of the Bible Belt. "I should be okay," he told himself.

"Should" is a funny little word that can have a whole lot of meaning attached to it. For example, I *should* be tall, dark, and slim and have a headful of hair. My kids *should* have lucrative jobs and pay dear old Dad's way for a change. Someone *should* tell the press that no one cares about Lindsay Lohan or Britney Spears, so they *should* stop reporting about them. Someone *should* tell Bruce Springsteen we don't give a crap about his political views, so he *should* shut up with his rants and just start making music. Likewise, Rudy's equipment *should* have been okay in the van for just one night, but a funny thing happened: The thieves that broke in didn't seem to understand the meaning of *should*. In the end, they entirely cleaned him out, relieving my good buddy of his guitar amplifier, effect pedals, cords, acoustic guitar, and two electric guitars, including his pride and joy, his black Les Paul, an instrument I remember well.

Back when Rudy got the idea that he needed a Les Paul, he went into search mode for the perfect one. Naïve as I was at the time, I said, "Dude, a Les Paul a Les Paul. Just buy one from whoever gives you the best price," but I knew there was no way he was going to do that, especially since he explained more than once that since they were handmade, every guitar had its own nuances. "They all play a bit differently, all sound a little different, so I've gotta find *my* guitar," he elaborated.

The search began, and we went to every music store within seventy-five miles. In each one, he sat there and played every Les Paul guitar he could get his hands on. When he didn't find the one he was looking for, we headed to another store. Of course there is no place on God's green Earth I'd rather be than in a music store, but I have to admit that even I got bored on that shopping excursion. Finally, in a little store on Race Street in Cincinnati, one that's long since been out of business, he found the instrument he was looking for.

One thing I haven't mentioned yet is that Rudy's haggling skills were second only to his playing skills. Once he found the perfect guitar, he was dead set on getting it at an acceptable price. He and the owner went around and around, till I was sure we were going to be tossed right out of the store. As a matter of fact, if that music store had had a bouncer, I am sure he would have been all over us. When they finally narrowed their negotiations down, Rudy told the owner, "Listen, man, this is all I've got in my wallet. I can't pay a cent more. Matter fact, if you make me pay that much, we won't even be able to get our car out of the parking garage. Cut me a break here, would ya?"

Much to my shock and awe, the guy smiled and gave Rudy his price, even knocking off enough to pay for parking. After the money and instrument exchanged hands, that sly Rudy opened his wallet, pulled out another twenty, and told the guy he wanted to buy a set of "extra super slinky" guitar strings. The owner shook his head, smiled, and gladly sold him the strings.

I have to admit, that Les Paul sounded and played incredible, so it was quite discouraging when those jerks took off with it years later in Nashville. Just imagine that young kid, new in town and among only strangers, all his stuff stolen and with nowhere to turn. Poor Rudy didn't even have so much as a harmonica to play at the first practice. He filed a police report and checked the pawn shops for a while, but his stuff never turned up. He ended up borrowing equipment from the band in Nashville until he could buy replacements, although I don't think he ever found another Les Paul. It would be nice if I could say all was well that ended well and that Rudy took Nashville by storm, but instead, the tour was canceled before the first gig, a sad story told elsewhere in this book.

A Cardboard Box for a Makeshift Drum

The Boy Scouts are pretty wise in their motto: "Be prepared." I never had the opportunity to be a Scout, as my parents didn't want to be bothered with it, but I strongly agree with this advice. As a musician, I find it particularly important to be prepared for anything and everything, to always expect the unexpected. I have personally adopted the attitude that Murphy was an extremely optimistic individual, especially when it pertains to a gig or recording session; of course, I'm this way about almost everything I do. I've just been burned way too many times, so nowadays, I'm more careful.

I enjoyed a twenty-five-year career in information technology (IT), and something I learned from that work is that if it is electrical, you can bet your bottom dollar that factory-installed smoke will find its way out, always at the most inopportune moment. While working in IT, I used to participate in tradeshows and exhibits quite often. I was always known as the one who not only brought extra stuff for myself but also to cover the stuff others would likely forget. Believe it or not, I'm not really all that anal retentive; it's just that experience has taught me that the nine-volt battery will die in your distortion pedal just before your Black Sabbath set.

Bearing this in mind, you should see the amount of stuff I take with me to gigs. Extra microphones and mic cables are a must, along with many, many guitar cables and enough extension cords to string the White House with Christmas lights. I usually take an extra amp head, tie wraps, and, of course, several rolls of rock 'n' roll tape, known to amateurs as duct tape. I don't leave home without an extra bass guitar and strings either. I didn't used to go to these lengths, but at one gig, I got so excited playing a bass solo on "Sweet Home Chicago" that I broke the top two strings on my six-string bass and had no spares. I had to retune using just E, A, and D. I really missed the B string but figured, *"Hey, G-strings are only needed by strippers in towns with decency laws!"*

Another thing I learned the hard way is that no one should ever—not even for a second—trust what the venue staff tells you about what equipment will be available onsite. My good friend and the best drummer I've ever jammed with, Jack Snow, was told he would have access to "a great set of drums," so there was no need for him to bring his. Thrilled that he didn't have to lug all his stuff in and out, he naïvely showed up at the gig drumless, only to find that the alleged "great set of drums" were buried in a closet on the other side of the building. Once he found all the pieces and set it up, he discovered that the kick drum pedal was broken and would not bounce back.

It made for an interesting gig, and it was kind of funny watching Jack struggle with that stubborn, inoperable pedal. Of course, that was not the first time Jack had to make do with what he had. Once, he even had to use a stuffed cardboard box as a kick drum on a recording, but he somehow made do.

When I was the band director for a large men's chorus, I was consistently told that the venue was equipped with a wonderful sound system. "Traveling groups use it all the time and appreciate it," they said. Upon arrival, I found a two-channel, quarter-inch input, RadioShack amp with a pair of homemade speaker cabinets, and two cheap Dynamic microphones. There were twenty-two guys in our group, so that measly selection just wasn't going to cut it. It took only once for that to happen before I started lugging my entire PA rig to every gig. If the venue did, in fact, have a nice system, I just left my stuff in the trailer, but I knew it was better to be prepared.

During a gig at a hall in northern Kentucky, I was playing bass, and my son was on guitar. I smelled smoke and noticed that the folks on the dance floor were pointing at the stage. Their eyes were wide, and some of them were covering their mouths with their hands. I turned around and saw flames rising out of my son's amp. I quickly ran over, beat out the flames, and grabbed the spare amp I'd brought.

If you've ever watched *The Red Green Show*, you know the importance of duct tape. This is doubly important in a band setting, and that's precisely why I refer to this wondrous creation as rock 'n' roll tape. Personally, I believe it is utterly impossible to put on a proper show without it, and any smart band will include it in their rider: Midas console, Audio-Technica microphones, QSC amps, EV speakers, 12 cases of Stella Artois, 2,000 green M&Ms, 2 limos, and 6 rolls of official 3M duct tape. How many gigs have been saved by duct-taping a busted drumhead? Maybe the more important question is: How many lawsuits have been avoided by duct-taping speaker wire or the snake in a high-traffic area, thus preventing unsuspecting passersby from tripping and breaking their necks?

For all you wireless proponents in this ever-connected generation, I suggest having a wired version of whatever you're using. You should take this as sound advice from someone who knows what He's talking about, as I provide technical support for microphones and wireless systems for a living. The vast majority of wireless microphones, body packs, and in-ear-monitors operate on the same frequencies as TV channels. With all the craziness the government caused with the digital TV mandate, wireless bandwidth is a hot commodity. The possibility of not being able to use your wireless system at any given venue is growing daily. Bring a wired mic and a couple floor wedges. If you choose to go wireless on your guitar, be prepared to stay tethered to your amp and accept the fact that you just might not be able turn backflips off the stage and run around in the crowd during that particular gig.

Perhaps we should talk the Boy Scouts into offering a merit badge for gig survival. I can see it now, a little, round badge with an amp on fire and Smokey the Bear saying, "Only you can prevent a bad gig!"

Sacrifices Made

I suppose it is apropos that I write about my dad today, just a few days before Father's Day. He has been gone for many years, but I still think about him every single day. He loved his kids and would do anything for us, and this story is yet another testament to the kind of selfless love he showed.

Dad was a musician, and it was from him that I picked up my love of music. Because of him, bluegrass gospel groups were always around our house, but on the rare occasions when we weren't graced with their presence, we could still find Dad sitting on the couch, playing his Gibson J45 Deluxe and belting out a country or gospel song. I think one reason I like *Brother, Where Art Thou?* so much is because I remember dad singing almost every song from that soundtrack. He had a really smooth, velvety voice and could croon Hank Williams better than everyone but Hank himself. He took pride in the fact that they were the same age and mentioned it often. By the time I was 4 or 5, I was already singing with Dad, and he took me with him to gigs at small churches so I could help him entertain the crowd. By the time I was 7 or 8, I was playing and accompanying him at his gigs as well.

Along with his love of music, I also picked up on Dad's family values. Nothing was more important to Dad than his family, except maybe his love for God. He was a hardworking man and made many personal sacrifices to make sure we had not only what we needed but also much of what we wanted.

By the time I was 12, I had discovered rock 'n' roll, and nothing else mattered to me. I had very little in the way of decent equipment, but I started playing out anyway. Some of the amps I showed up with for jam sessions were quite embarrassing. My father absolutely hated rock 'n' roll and had no reservations whatsoever about saying so. He had dreams of me being onstage at the Grand Ole Opry, but once I discovered rock, that dream fell by the wayside. Even though he despised the music I chose to play, maybe as much as I despise disco, Dad knew I still needed the equipment to play it. Many-a-father might have just said, "Boy, you're on your own," to a son who went against his wishes, but that was not my dad.

Dad worked the dayshift at the post office annex in Cincinnati, putting in his long days of tedious work after long commutes to get there, followed by long commutes home. Back then, the post office didn't exactly pay a boatload of money, but it was a decent living. Seemingly out of nowhere, he started working the nightshift as a security guard, while keeping his day job at the post office. I just assumed times were tough and that he needed the extra money for bills, but I couldn't have been more wrong. The truth was that Dad took that extra job so he could earn enough to buy me a new bass amplifier to gig with. As soon as he saved up enough cash, he quit the second job and bought me a really nice piggyback bass amp, something I still own to this day. I can't think of many fathers who would do such a thing for their children, and it simply blows my mind.

This Sunday, as another Father's Day rolls by, I think I'll pull out that old amp, play a song for Dad, and just hope I'm half the father or even half the man he was.

How Many Blondes Does It Take To Park a Van?

Showtime, my friend Jack's band, were top-forty players, as I mentioned, but they also played some country. They really specialized in show tunes. With such a wide variety of music styles to offer, Showtime needed a lot of members. In addition to their rhythm section, they had a horn section, as well as three female back-up vocalists. With all due respect, those ladies weren't exactly the sharpest tools in the shed, and this story is primarily about them.

Having such a large band presented a problem when it came to hauling equipment. For several years, Showtime just used whatever trucks or vans they could find. As they became more successful, they decided to invest in a vehicle to carry their equipment. After an extensive search, they settled on a brand new panel van. It was something like a bread truck, a very tall cargo vehicle with enough room for them to build shelves on the sides, a perfect setup.

The backups were real lookers and an extremely talented trio of singers, but as I said, they weren't very bright. The very first gig the band played after purchasing their truck was at an upscale hotel in Cincinnati. The hotel lounge was known for hosting up-and-coming bands. Jack said their manager worked really hard to land them the spot, so Showtime was happy to get the gig and ready to give a great performance. On the day of the show, all the male band members had to work and drive straight from their jobs to the venue. Thus, they decided the best course of action was to load the truck the night before, then let the three girls drive it to the gig. Of course they proved their blondeness in short order.

The girls had no trouble driving the truck or locating the venue. In fact, they even arrived early, about a half-hour before the band. They decided to surprise the guys by pulling up to the door and getting a head start on unloading the equipment. What happened next can be summed up in one short phrase: ten-foot-tall truck with a nine-foot-high overhang.

The damage to the new van was almost unfathomable. The girls must have been doing twenty-five miles per hour when they hit that overhang, because they damn near took the top clean off the truck and tore the overhang to shreds. Oh, the horror of the band guys when they rounded the bend and saw the carnage! It is fairly safe to say that Showtime was not invited to that particular hotel for a return engagement.

Kicking In To Buy Equipment

This subject should conjure up a whole host of bad memories and make you shudder with dread. Just thinking about it should make your blood boil. Kicking in to buy equipment? How stupid could anyone be? I don't want to rub salt in your wounds or try to sound as if I'm smarter than the rest of you, but I've never fallen into that trap. However, I know many, many musicians who have, and I'd venture to say that some of you who are reading this are among them. I just recognize the possible danger and have always managed to steer clear of that bad decision, but allow me to explain the issue for the non-musician reader who is asking, "What's so wrong with pooling your money to buy big-ticket items? After all, the entire band will use it, right?" On the surface, it does sound logical, but I cannot tell you how dangerous it is, and it will most definitely lead to fights and damaged relationships.

For most bands, sharing would involve PA equipment and possibly a few lights. For some, it may also include vans or trucks and, in this age of technology, even computers and video equipment. Bands also may set aside money for studio time and travel expenses. As you can see, a lot of finances can be tied up in shared resources. So what's the problem? Well, to answer that question, let me ask you a couple of my own: What do you do if someone leaves the band or the band splits up? Can you see the issue now?

It's a bit easier to handle a single person leaving the band than it is to deal with the entire band breaking up. If an individual takes off, you can usually figure out how much that person put in and just return that amount to them, although things can get weird in a hurry when you start talking depreciation or if they actually want hardware. It's far more difficult to manage the dispersion of equipment and/or money when the whole band crumbles. Do you sell everything and split the cash? Do you divvy up equipment among the members? If so, how do you split up a PA, and why would you? The difficulties are endless in such a situation. I'm not even sure King Solomon could figure that one out.

Let me share a real-life story about my brother's band. Like me, Andy is a bass player, and he's spent many years playing in bluegrass and country bands. There is something you should know about bluegrass pickers: They are a crazy bunch, and they don't ever want to quit playing. Most will play anywhere, anytime, even all night long. When the band calls for practice, their wives can count on sleeping alone that night, because it's almost always an all-nighter. They go to bluegrass festivals not to listen to the bands onstage but to jam in the parking lot with other musicians who also didn't show up to hear the other bands. They get as drunk as monkeys on good beer and play gospel music. Despite the talent level of a player, the rest of the musicians will adjust to make sure everyone fits in. I guarantee that you will never find any artist as devoted to his or her craft as a bluegrass picker. Truly, Bill Monroe can be proud of what he created.

Andy hooked up with some local guys to play some bluegrass and a little country. It didn't take long for them to get ready for the gig, but they did need a PA system. All the guys had good jobs and decided to pitch in to buy what they needed, and they weren't cheap about it either. They bought a nice powered console, a couple stick speakers, very decent microphones, and stands, cables, and other accessories. Like I said, it cost them more than a few pretty pennies, but it served them well.

Like almost all bands do, that one eventually split up, albeit not in the usual way. Instead of a blowup, they experienced more of a fizzle-out; in other words, they all got too busy with work and family, and gigs and practices became fewer and fewer, until they just didn't play anymore. After a good while, Andy called the assumed leader of the band and asked about the possibility of taking possession of some of the equipment. In reply, he received a lot of doubletalk and rambling, but it basically boiled down to him being told that the gear just seemed to waltz off and that the leader claimed he had no idea where it was. Andy decided not to push the issue, even though he knew he was being lied to. To make matters worse, he joined another band

and went through an almost identical situation, though, to my brother's credit, the second time could be summed up as a bit of scam by someone he went to church with, which was why he chose not to make an issue out of that event either. After all, church folks are supposed to be trustworthy, right? Anyway, that's a story for another chapter.

Mama always said I'm the best-looking of her children, but she secretly told me I'm the smartest as well. Those incidents proved it, because I would never let myself get caught up in such a thing, especially not twice. In all the bands I've worked with, I've always insisted that band members buy individual components of the shared equipment. That way, if anyone leaves or if the band breaks up, those who depart can just take with them whatever they bought. It may sound like an odd arrangement, but it works, and I've never lost any money in a band split. See? Mama was right about me being the smartest! Of course she was also right about the best-looking, but there is no sense in stating the obvious.

A Warm Body with a Pulse

I am writing this story mainly for the benefit of FOH engineers in church settings, although I'm sure just about everyone in any venue can sympathize with their plight. I had a hard time trying to decide where to place this story. It easily could have fit in "Personnel" or "Gigs from Down Under," but since it deals with the folks who handle the sound systems, I decided the "Equipment" section is a good place for it.

So let's talk about the church FOH engineer. I talk to these people every day in my job as the manager of a technical support group at a major microphone company, and all I can say is that in general, they seem to be a great bunch of guys. I have found that the experience and knowledge among house of worship (HOW) FOH engineers varies quite broadly. In very large churches, you may find FOH engineers with lots of experience. Many have been on the road with major rock 'n' roll acts and have worked in venues ranging from large clubs to stadiums. Every time I speak to one on the phone, I learn something. A lot of ex-rockers from back in the day now sit behind the consoles in many churches. They have great ears and a fair amount of technical knowledge, but many have been away from the business for a while. In smaller churches, the sound guys often land the job simply on the premise that they have a warm body and a pulse to offer. Sometimes, it was because they just so happened to be standing too close to the mixing console when someone was needed. I really feel for these sound guys, because as much as they want to do a great job, few know much about the audio they're tasked with manning. They are desperate to learn but have very limited resources, and many don't know where to turn for help. When I talk to them, I find that they are among the most appreciative customers who call in.

FOH engineers in both the secular and the HOW audio world are very important to the quality of the audio experience, but I have to say the secular folks really have it made when compared to the church guys, at least in the area of respect. Let me lay this out for you: Quite often, the sound guy at a church, particularly a small church, has only inadequate or antiquated equipment to work with and little to no budget, forcing him to beg for, borrow, or steal what he needs. Many churches, perhaps even most these days, operate by committee, and these committees know nothing about audio. Instead of listening to the sound guy and trusting any expertise he does happen to have, committees prefer to yield to the recommendation of the member whose nephew works at RadioShack and can get them a deal. This really happens, folks!

You will also find that aesthetics always win over good audio. I've seen mixing consoles set up in closed rooms with one window, and the FOH engineers who work there are expected to mix the service via headphones. At best, the console is placed at the very back in the corner of the room, where sound reflects everywhere. I once visited a small church that placed their column PA cabinets horizontally under the front pew, facing forward, simply because the congregation didn't want to look at speakers. Not only did it sound horrible, but there were horrible feedback issues as well.

One common factor among these valiant individuals, though, is that there are few people more dedicated to the task at hand. I'd venture to say that a great majority of them put in more time than the pastor. Very often, they spend their own money on batteries, CDs, SPL meters, and technical manuals. Most assuredly, they dig deep into their own piggybanks if there just so happens to be a training session in town. They are the first to arrive at church on Sunday mornings and the last to leave. They are there every service, in attendance at every special event. When I see those humorous beer commercials about unsung heroes, I can't help but think that these guys should be the subjects of the next ad: "Hey, you, Mr. Got-Caught-Standing-Too-Close-to-the-Mixing-Console…"

Is This Thing on?

It never ceases to amaze me that some musicians see no need to learn anything about the equipment they use to make their living. It seems to make logical sense that one should at least know something about the basics and general maintenance of those devices that allow them to practice their chosen craft. Would you hire a plumber who knows nothing about a soldering torch? A truck driver who knows how to handle the road but doesn't know that he occasionally has to put fuel in the gas tank? What about a guy who's invested countless hours to train for sky-diving, but only after jumping out of the plane does he realize he was supposed to check that the parachute was actually packed? Perhaps you've heard the story about the CEO baffled by a paper shredder. When the young engineer walks by and asks, "Sir, do you need help," the CEO answers, "Well, my administrative assistant is out for the day, and I have this very sensitive document here. It needs to be taken care of immediately." The engineer smiles, turns on the shredder, and places the document on the input tray, then watches it disappear. "Great! Can you make another? I need two copies," the foolish CEO declares, much to the worker's horror. Every professional in every trade is expected to know about the tools they use or, at the very least, pay a competent person to handle those things. Failing to do so will place the business and their career in great jeopardy. It's a bit disheartening that most in the business world are aware of this, while too many musicians remain comfortably clueless about some or all of their gear.

Does a musician need to know how to trace a circuit on a printed circuit board or what companding algorithms are used by their wireless microphone systems? Of course not, but every musician should know some of the basics, such as what hooks to what and why. In my job as a Contact Center manager for a microphone company, I hear stories all day long about the things people do—or, probably more appropriately, don't do—that cause them problems during a gig. I do applaud those folks who call in so they can learn, but I get a real charge out of those who think they already know the answer, yet they expect us to perform some type of magic to fix what they screwed up. In reality, it's actually quite hard to put that factory-installed smoke back in once someone has let it escape.

A very close friend shared the following story with me about a performance he witnessed in South Carolina, and I think it's worth repeating. Sam was visiting his family back in the old country, and he decided to take them to a country music/comedy show at a place called The Barn. It really was just a barn at one time, but it had been very nicely converted into a

dinner theater. The venue served up good Southern cooking and live country

music performances, as well as corny stand-up comics. The local old folks

loved the place, but it was also a hot spot for tourists. As for décor, just

picture a Cracker Barrel restaurant on steroids. Old farm equipment,

washboards, jugs, license plates from the forties and fifties, and other relics

adorned the whole place. The menu consisted of fried chicken, country ham,

mashed potatoes, cornbread, and just about any fried or starchy edible a

person could want, the kind of food that clogged the arteries as diners

enjoyed every savory bite.

On one particular evening, there was a father, daughter, and son

band playing a guitar, banjo, and upright bass respectively; of course, since it

was country or bluegrass music, I suppose it could be called doghouse bass.

They were very entertaining and as stereotypically backwoods as they could

get, right down to Dad's bib overalls and his daughter's Elly May pigtails.

They didn't need a comedian that night because the band was a hoot on its

own. The audience could see every joke coming from a mile away, but they

delivered them so well that they were still funny.

Halfway through their first song, Sam noticed that their music

sounded very hollow, always just on the edge of suffering from feedback.

That didn't really make sense, because they had a great sound system, and

they were using an Audio-Technica AT4033 side-address studio microphone,

one of the best on the market. Upon closer inspection, Sam noticed that it was positioned backward, so they were actually singing and playing into the null area, with the sweet spot pointing out at the audience. He was totally amazed and wondered how they had managed to get it so wrong. In spite of their corny jokes, twangs, and country garb, they seemed professional enough, and they should have known how to properly use their equipment, but they obviously didn't.

After the band's first set, Sam walked backstage and talked with the dad during the break. He mentioned how much he liked the show, then told the guy, "Please forgive me for butting in, but I work for the company that makes the microphone you are using. Do you know you've been singing into the back of it?"

The hillbilly stared at him in total embarrassment and said, "Really? I thought something was wrong, because everyone I talked to said it's the best mic to use. I thought maybe the PA was broke." He then walked back onstage and casually turned the microphone around. Of course it screamed feedback, and he had to turn the gain down, but the rest of the show sounded great. He just smiled at Sam from the stage for the rest of the night, and if Sam's wife wasn't there, I am sure the guy would have offered him his daughter's hand in marriage, probably armed with a shotgun all the while.

Hey, Man, You've Gotta Take Care of Your Stuff

I'm really sorry for this, but it's time for me to get really preachy,

though it won't have anything to do with religion. Before I do, though, I need

to attempt to educate some of the more mentally challenged musicians among

us about a concept called stewardship. For you drummers, that's spelled S-T-

E-W-A-R-D-S-H-I-P, and it's pronounced *'stü-ǝrd-ˌship*. It can be defined as

"the careful and responsible management of something entrusted to one's

care," and it applies to many, many things. Quite often, stewardship is used in

reference to money, but it is applicable to far more than your paycheck. In

these modern times, one very common reference to it is in relationship to the

environment. God bless those tree-huggers! In the BigBassMan dictionary,

stewardship means "to take good care of the stuff that's been given to you

because you probably didn't earn it yourself and, chances are, when it's gone,

you won't get any replacements." Now that that's out of the way, let me get

on with my sermon.

Denny Horgan is a fire-and-brimstone, old-line Pentecostal evangelist/preacher, but he is also a musician. Actually, his entire family consists of good musicians, and he has made their band part of his show; I call it that rather than a ministry because I firmly believe that what Denny does is more about being a theatrical performance than it is about giving back to God. For a typical Horgan show, they usually bring in their own PA equipment and their own sound guy, but for one particular performance, I was asked to run sound for them using the house sound system at the church. I nearly laughed out loud as I watched Denny jump from the stage and land on the first pew with one foot on the seat and the other on the back. The poor old lady in the second row looked up at him like he was a stripper at a Chippendales dance revue, like she didn't know if is she should shout halleluiah or slip her offering money into his drawers.

Denny is also a real screamer, and the problem that night was that he went from a soft whisper to a horrendous, bloodcurdling shriek in a fraction of a second, all while in the air on the way to the first pew. I desperately needed a compressor/limiter with a hard knee limit set, but instead, I had to ride the console fader like a rodeo cowboy on a bull, in an attempt to maintain an acceptable sound level, and I had very little success. There was just no way to know when the guy was going to explode. I'm also fairly confident in saying he's never actually finished a sermon, because at some point, he inevitably stops and shouts, "I feel a healing coming on!" The service then launches into a slobber-fest, with all kinds of wailing and gnashing of teeth at the altar.

As I mentioned, all the Horgan's are very fine singers and musicians. They play way too much Southern gospel to suit my taste, but even I can admit that they are talented. The stuff Denny supposedly writes is always fairly hokey, but at least they play it well. At one particular event, the church brought the Horgan show in for a one-night stand, and I was asked to provide help with their setup. I've been in and around many bands and have seen many things, but I could only stand there in shock and horror as I watched their team. First, they removed the church's equipment from the stage, and I had never seen such reckless disregard for other people's belongings in my entire career as musician and audio engineer. They literally just threw the equipment in a backroom or dragged it in and kicked it aside. The gear abuse was so bad that I actually stopped them and advised them that I would gladly move whatever they did not want onstage. Their bus driver, who also just so happened to be their sound guy and their merch table sales agents, gave me one of those who-the-heck-do-you-think-you-are-mister? looks, but I eventually managed to clear the stage.

When they started hauling in their stuff, I was stunned again. They clearly had no shame in mistreating other people's things, but that did not even compare with the battering their equipment received. None of the amps or PA cabinets had covers, the console lacked a case, there was no front or back cover on their amp racks, the cables were wadded up and carelessly

shoved into plastic tubs in knots, and the instruments were stashed in thin,

cheap gig bags. To make matters worse, the stuff was just stacked

haphazardly in their truck, in no particular order. They actually had some

really nice equipment, but it was beaten to death from the abuse of them

spending forty-plus weeks a year on the road, going from church to church

and tent revival to tent revival without ever properly packing it away. Every

cabinet suffered from ugly dings and missing chunks, the grill cloth was

hanging off the speakers, several channels on the console were inoperable,

and most of the cables were plagued with shorts. It was unbelievable, enough

to give an audio engineer a heart attack.

After swapping out various cables, the Horgan's managed to get

things up and running with only a few hums and buzzes. I was equally

amazed and appalled by the equipment carnage I had witnessed, but it was

their stuff, so I figured they could treat it however they wanted. My opinion

about that changed a bit when they set up their merchandise table.

Of course they had stacks of records and tapes for sale, but they also

had the audacity to set out a collection basket, with a sign requesting

donations to help them replace some of their music equipment. At that point,

someone nearly had to hold me down, because I was absolutely livid. The

idiots had beaten the crap out of their stuff, yet they expected the good

people of the congregation to replace it. They wanted little old church ladies to fork over their Social Security checks so they could buy more equipment to abuse and destroy. That preacher man needs to read that Bible he preaches from, especially the parts about stewardship.

I firmly believe anyone who lives off the donations of others must use those charitable contributions wisely. Needless to say, I didn't put a penny in their basket, and I will never again attend a Horgan show.

Almost Beaten Up Buying a PA

What kind of equipment did your first band have? The best money can buy, I'm sure. Not! Did your guitar player have stacks of Marshalls and a brand new Les Paul? Did your bass player have a Rickenbacker with dual Ampeg amps? What about the drummer? I bet he sat behind a double-set of chrome Slingerlands, and of course, I'm sure you had a stack of concert PA speakers with a thirty-two channel board. I do hope you're picking up my sarcasm here, because I'm laying it on real thick. If your first band was anything like most, you probably had a bunch of mismatched crap. In my first real band, if I can even call it that, I played rhythm guitar. That instrument came from a Western Auto hardware store. My amp was a third-hand, no-name practice variety; I thought I was ready for a concert tour after borrowing a Sears Silvertone guitar amp. Our drummer had a hodgepodge to play with, all different makes and colors, and his cymbals were just a half-step above pie pans. Our lead guitarist had the closest thing to real equipment, although he played out of a bass amp instead of a guitar amp.

As is the case for many garage band startups, the real issue for us was our PA system. Also like most bands, we started out using Dynamic microphones running through our individual guitar amps. Given the fact that our guitar amps didn't have the balls necessary to drive the guitar alone, not to mention a microphone, our vocals suffered greatly. Our first standalone PA system consisted of an ancient Fanon two-input amp and a pair of columns that I built, each with a pair of RadioShack ten-inch speakers. I reused the same columns later, replacing the speakers with floodlights for makeshift lighting, but that's a story for another day.

As we upgraded our personal gear over time, it became quite clear that my homemade PA just wasn't cutting it; in fact, it never really had. Being in the dire straits we found ourselves in, we began looking for a more suitable system. A few trips to the local music stores were enough to convince us that a new PA was out of the question, so we started looking for a used one. It wouldn't be such a big deal today, thanks to the invention of the internet, Amazon, and EBay, but back then, it required perusing the classifieds, buying a *Trading Post,* and checking ads on bulletin boards. It was no easy task, and we found ourselves driving all over town looking at mostly blown-up, torn-up, or overpriced PA systems. As frustrating as it was, we hung in there and finally ran across what looked like a nice PA at a reasonable price.

We jumped into two cars and headed across the Ohio River, to the east side of Cincinnati. Since I had no idea where we were going, I followed

Charlie, our drummer. Even though he claimed to know the way, it became quite obvious from his erratic lane changes and occasional turnabouts that he had no idea where we were heading. If it happened today, I would have been on the cell phone yelling at him, but back then, all I could do was ride his bumper and hope he didn't run any red lights. I was driving a 1972 Ford Torino, which just so happened to be the coolest car on the planet at the time. The thing had a lot of leg room, and guys were constantly asking to borrow my keys so they could take their chicks out for extracurricular activities. So many guys had used my car for a little last-minute lovin' that they wanted to enshrine the back seat after I wrecked the thing. I know this has nothing to do with the story, but I do love to brag about that car, yet another piece of equipment that really served me and others well.

After driving around the neighborhood for some time, Charlie determined at the last minute that he needed to make a left at the next light, so he suddenly changed lanes. I had no alternative but to change lanes as well, and I cut off a pickup in the process. The driver of the truck blew his horn at us, which was to be expected, but everything would have turned out all right if Ronnie, our bass player, had resisted the urge to flip the angry driver off.

We get caught at the light, and the truck whipped over into the lane next to us. The furious man behind the wheel started yelling at Ronnie, who responded with a great big, "Eff you!" The other driver jumped out in a rage and headed straight for Ronnie's door. He looked like a cross between a

Chicago Bears linebacker and a professional wrestler, and he was ready to kick the ever-loving crap out of our bass player. He left his truck in gear, though, and it started to roll, causing his abandoned wife to scream at him from the passenger seat. Ronnie leaned toward me, frantically trying to roll up the window and lock the door. When the guy took a swing at Ronnie, his fist crashed into the window hard; to this day, I have no idea why it didn't shatter into a million tiny pieces.

Meanwhile, Charlie watched the scene unfold through his rearview mirror, and he figured it was best if we all got the hell out of Dodge in a hurry. He blew his horn to get my attention, then ran the red light. I floored it as well, leaving the angry driver to chase after his still-rolling truck and frantic wife.

Two or three blocks beyond that, we arrived at our destination. Ronnie just sat there, white as a sheet, while the guys in the other car jumped out and yelled, "What the hell was that about?" Of course I replied, "Your crazy driving and Ronnie's big mouth damn near got my butt kicked!" After we all settled down, we went in and bought the Peavey PA system, which sounded fantastic.

I've been in bar fights at gigs. I've experienced other musicians throwing cymbals at me during practice. I've even almost electrocuted myself using hacked equipment, but that was the first and only time I was almost killed trying to buy music equipment, as long as you don't count all the times

my wife found out about how much I actually paid for new equipment.

Yes, Alcohol Was Involved

Not Our Free Beer!

I would imagine that most musicians dearly love *The Blues Brothers*, a classic film with great music, a hilarious script, and fabulous acting. They certainly couldn't have chosen a better cast, and my computer is loaded with sound bites from the movie. I smile every time I hear, "We're on a mission from God," or, "Four fried chickens and a Coke." There is one scene in particular that resonates with me because it closely resembles an experience I shared with my band.

I've already mentioned Stonehenge several times. We were a four-member, hard rock 'n' roll band back in the early to mid-seventies. We were very serious about three things: music, women, and drinking. The music part was obvious. We practiced at least two nights a week and played every Friday and Saturday night. People still talk about our Black Sabbath renditions, and we've been told more than once, "They were right on!" From time to time, I get a Facebook or Classmates message from someone who knew me back then, and they still talk to me about Stonehenge. Most are happy but somewhat surprised to find I'm still playing. My online photos are a giveaway, even though I've traded my long hair and skinny waist for a shaved head and healthy belly. At the risk of sounding arrogant, there is no doubt that Stonehenge was an excellent band. Our guitar player could burn up the frets, and I could (and still can) belt out some blues. We also had an amazing stage presence.

The women part also goes without saying. After all, we were musicians, and women are a byproduct of playing in a band. That may sound sexist, but as Larry the Cable Guy would say, "Lord, I'm sorry for saying that…and please be with them starving Pygmies down there in New Guinea." It is undeniable that women follow bands, and band members are all too ready to welcome their fangirls. I confess that even outside the band, each and every member was always on the prowl for a hot babe, and I'm so ashamed…not!

Drinking was more than a hobby for our band and all our friends. It was, in fact, a way of life. I can honestly say there wasn't an amateur drinker among us. I'm not proud of this in the least, but I actually overdosed on alcohol and almost pulled a Jimi Hendrix and choked on my own puke. Real glamorous, huh? It is difficult to even explain how much beer our band could consume, but that's really the subject of this story. That *Blues Brothers* scene I referred to a moment ago took place in a country bar, and I still think it ranks as one of the funniest scenes in any movie ever made. At the end, the bar owner pays them and presents them with their bar tab, only to reveal that they drank more than what they made. I must admit that I can absolutely identify, and maybe that's why I love the movie so much.

We took a gig as the house band at a really sleazy club in Newport, Kentucky. The club owner offered us a fairly nice amount, but he also agreed to provide beer for free. The guy had absolutely no idea what he was in for in that regard. We drank more beer than we could carry, and that was when *we* were paying for it, so you can imagine what we could consume when it was on the house.

The first night, we showed up, set up, ordered our first round, and started playing. I felt so sorry for the waitress. She looked like a hod carrier trying to keep four brick layers busy with bricks and cement. At the end of the night, the club owner walked up to us as we were sitting around having one more for the road. Without batting an eye, he exclaimed, "You guys drink too damn much. There's no way I can keep you in beer. Hell, you drank away all my profits for the night!" We looked up at him like kids caught with our hands in the cookie jar. I guess he saw the shock on our faces, because he told us he would still provide our beer for half-price from that point forward. All things considered, that was still rather nice of him, and at least he didn't take it out of our pay.

Passed Out After the First Set

Like most people, I've done a lot of things in my life that I'm not proud of. Actually, there are many things I regret, things I'm flat out ashamed of and embarrassed to even talk about, but very few of those transgressions occurred during musical performances. To me, the gig must be pure and should be viewed as a sacred thing. I would never do anything to jeopardize the music or the performance, because the crowd, the band, and the music deserve the best I can put forward. I know that might sound a bit self-righteous, but I do try to live by that credo. I also believe that once a musician steps onstage, it's no longer all about that musician. As entertainers, we are there for the audience, so it is all about them, right from the very first note. Nothing bugs me more than going to a concert or a club and seeing the band interact with each other, joke with one another, then turn their backs on the audience, doing little or nothing to engage them, almost as if they're still in a basement or garage, doing their own private jam session, only occasionally casting the crowd glances as if to say, *"Oh, hey! Sure, you guys can watch if you want."*

A couple years ago, I judged a Battle of the Bands, and I really dinged bands for that very thing. Even if the band danced and moved about the stage like crazy people, and even if they choreographed their show, they lost points

if they did not engage the audience. Even worse—and the only unpardonable

sin onstage, in my opinion—is to get drunk or stoned before or during a live

performance. Too many musicians claim, "Man, I play so much better when

I'm high. I feel loose, more in tune with the music, and that really helps me

get in a groove!" Sure, let them keep telling themselves that, but the honest

truth is that they only *think* they play better. In most cases, the audience

would beg to differ.

The bass player in our band back in the seventies often committed

that carnal sin of getting drunk during our gigs, and he played quite poorly

after just a few drinks. In a biker bar once, I heard some really bad bass notes

coming from the left side of the stage. I glanced over just in time to see our

bass man collapsing against the wall, almost passing out. At the time, I was

the lead singer, not on guitar for that particular song, so I ran over, snatched

the bass out of his hand, and finished the tune. I ended up playing bass for

the rest of the night, because he was too wasted to even return to the stage. It

turned out okay, since I was really a better player anyway, although some of

the songs were a little thin without a rhythm guitar. Needless to say, we gave

him four kinds of hell at the next practice.

A very bad thing happened a couple months later at the same biker

bar, something that really made me look like a hypocrite. As I mentioned

earlier, I was the lead singer of that band, but I was also the only singer. We played a lot of very hard rock 'n' roll, which was not exactly easy on the vocal

cords. To add insult to injury, I smoked like a freight train, upward of two

packs of Viceroys a day. For club gigs, we usually played Friday and Saturday

nights back to back, and my voice was shot after four or five hours of

Sabbath and the like. I could usually get through the Fridays okay, but

Saturdays were always tough. I tried everything under the sun to restore my

voice, from throat lozenges to gargling with salt water, but nothing seemed to

help. Eventually, I found another home remedy: tequila. For some reason, it

always cleared up my voice and allowed me to finish the night. I won't give

medical advice here, but I can honestly say it helped in my case.

Once I knew about the healing power of that elixir, I kept a double-

shot of tequila onstage beside me at all times, just in case. One of the great

things about being the lead singer of the band is that folks in the audience like

to buy the front man drinks. They told the bartenders, "Send up another of

whatever he's drinkin'!" Being the nice guy I am, I couldn't possibly refuse

such kind gestures. As I said, I don't ever want to jeopardize a gig, but one

night, I really let my guard down. I don't know if it was the place, because

that particular bar was a real party, or if it was because my throat hurt more

than usual, but either way, I was fully slammed by the end of the first set.

Folks sent me drinks one after another, and I continued throwing back all

that tequila without even thinking; it didn't help that I absolutely love it, my

own personal Isildur's Bane.

Anyway, after the first set, I stumbled out into the parking lot and passed out on the hood of my car. After a few minutes, a couple good-looking biker babes carried me in and stood me up in front of my microphone. I managed to sing, even totally in a fog, but there was no way I could play guitar. I did, in fact, feel really loose, but I can't guarantee that the vocals were any better than usual. As a matter of fact, I don't even know for sure that I sang the correct words. After running around the stage for a while, sweating like a pig and out of tequila, I managed to sober up just enough to finish the gig, albeit with a monster headache.

Of course I'm a hypocrite for yelling at Ronnie for his overindulgence, but I can honestly say that was the first and last time I ever got drunk during a gig. I can't say the same for Ronnie though.

Barfunkonium

"WHAT WE'RE GONNA DO IS GO BACK, WAY BACK, BACK

INTO TIME, When the ONLY PEOPLE that EXISTED WERE

TROGLODYTES..." Sorry, but I've been listening to the oldies station again,

and that silly song was playing. There were some great tunes back in the day,

but that wasn't one of them, and now I can't get the tune out of my head!

Unless you're still a kid yourself, I do want to take you back a whole bunch of

years, though, back to your first couple years of high school. Remember how

much you dreaded, maybe hated, or, as in my case, absolutely loathed physics

class with every ounce of your being? While you're remembering, do you

recall that short, dumpy, bitchy, old physics teacher, the only one during your

entire four or five years of high school who gave homework over Christmas

vacation, the teacher who never once received even one vote for Teacher of

the Year? I'm curious to know just how long you spent on the periodic table

during that class from hell. I think my class was introduced to that godawful

thing the first week of September, and it was still staring us in the face in May.

I'm sure by now you are wondering what, in the name of Black Sabbath's third album, the periodic table could possibly have to do with musicians, other than the fact that they both involve heavy metal. The answer is quite simple, but please bear with me as I explain.

There is an elusive element that does not show up on that miserable periodic table, one only musicians can identify. In fact, I'm quite certain that none actually realize the significance of this knowledge. They do not realize that any one of them could announce the discovery of this substance and find themselves in the running for the Nobel Prize in physics. Just what is this mysterious substance? I will gladly take my place alongside the many Nobel laureates and take full credit for the discovery of—drumroll please—barfunkonium.

Just what is barfunkonium, and why is it significant and known only to musicians? Well, it is that nasty, awful, clingy smell and film you find on your clothes and equipment the day after a gig. Barfunkonium is composed of many substances, including smoke (of cigarette, cigar, and sometimes weed origins), body odor, urine, beer and whiskey, cheap perfume and aftershave, and Lord only knows what else. I'm convinced that the stuff is toxic. If Homeland Security knew about it, I'm sure the terror threat level would be raised a color or two. I would not be a bit surprised to find that barfunkonium would register on a Geiger counter. I envision a small room deep underground, within the bowels of the Centers for Disease Control in Atlanta, where all hazardous materials are studied. Several masked scientists are probably there right now, researching barfunkonium right this minute, in the hopes of finding an antidote for its exposure.

All musicians can identify with the way this stuff sticks to your skin and clothes, and any fabric afflicted with it must be immediately thrown in the washing machine, to be laundered in the hottest water possible, perhaps through more than one cycle with an extra cup of Tide. Your body must be cleansed of this stinking rot as soon as you return home from a gig. If not, the barfunkonium will transfer to your bed, your sofa, or anything else you touch. Do you think your wife will get near you, much less want to be intimate, while you are basking in the afterglow of a barfunkonium assault? Have you ever left your gear in the van or truck and unloaded it the next day? As we say down South, Lord, have mercy! The smell will actually gag a maggot! For this very reason, no matter how tired I was, I always tried to unload the van and wipe down my equipment the night of the gig, even while my gear and I were still under the effect of barfunkonium.

For a while, I was in a classic rock band that played biker bars on occasion. During that time, I also played bass for a contemporary church service on Sunday mornings. I opened my bass guitar case one Sunday morning, and the barfunkonium rushed from the case and filled the air around the stage. All the ex-club musicians immediately recognized the stench and knew where I'd been playing, because it is the kind of aroma you will never forget, like when I got off the plane in Caracas, Venezuela a few years ago and walked into the overwhelming nostril invasion of leaded gas. I had

not smelled those fumes since my teens, but I immediately recognized them.

Likewise, those ex-bar musicians knew and judged me for my sins, the

pompous, arrogant, holier-than-thou jerks! I bet they had some really unholy

thoughts when that barfunkonium ambushed their nostrils. Smell is one of

the strongest memory-joggers known to man, so I'm sure their hypocritical

minds went on several journeys they shouldn't have when they took in that

all-too-familiar scent.

Not only does barfunkonium give off a terrible smell, but there is

also a greasy film associated with it. It attacks clothing, case linings, and even

the Tolex on amplifiers. You can actually see this nasty coating lurking on

your guitar, so thick you can write your name in it with your finger. Left

alone, I'm quite certain it would remove the finish from the guitar and cause

early dry rot of your guitar case lining. I've given a lot of thought to

proposing this to the WD-40 folks as a possible new ingredient to help

remove rust from lug nuts.

I have studied the periodic table for available element notations.

Therefore, as the recipient of this year's Nobel Prize for physics, I dub the

newly discovered element barfunkonium as BF, and it shall be placed at

Number 119 on said table. Thank you! Thank you very much!

Fifteen Drunk Japanese and the Karaoke King

I have been a performer for fifty years, half a century! I can hardly believe I've been behind microphones and in front of crowds for that long. Since I was 5 years old, when my father stood me onstage in front of a church congregation, I've known how to work an audience. I've gone from church gigs to school dances to wedding receptions to biker bars to clubs and, finally, on to concert stages, and I've treated each and every gig like it was the biggest of my lifetime. If there's a microphone, a guitar, and at least one person in the audience, my performance button is turned on, and I'm ready to shout, "Hit it!" Even though I no longer perform for a living, I still play regularly, mostly in churches and at benefits. My day gig is, without a doubt, the best possible job for a recovering musician, somewhat of a false term, since none of us ever fully recover and don't really want to. As I've mentioned, I work for a microphone manufacturer, providing technical support for microphones and wireless systems. I've often joked that my job is to babysit rock stars, but that is actually part of it, a part I enjoy. I also love to work with studio engineers and weekend warriors, helping them choose and use the best mics for their application. I have some very jealous friends who call me up at work and find me in the studio playing guitar to test a new microphone. It sure beats the heck out of digging ditches!

Recently, I was sent to Japan, the home of our corporate headquarters, to work with a global team on a project. The Japanese have their own way of conducting business, at least in my company. We sat in a conference room all day, longing for air-conditioning, listening to dull presentations. Afterward, we headed out and sat on the floor, ate sushi, and drank beer for half the night. It was during that time that we actually conducted the real business. As a side note, I must tell you that you have not eaten real sushi until you have had it in Japan. One night, they brought a basketful, and I swear one of the fishtails was still wiggling, its gills still flapping. Talk about fresh sushi!

On that particular trip, after the second night of sushi and lots of beer, it was suggested that we partake in a little karaoke. I'd always thought it was a stereotype that the Japanese like karaoke, but it is apparently true. About fifteen Japanese, three Americans, one Brit, and a couple guys from Singapore, all more than slightly inebriated, headed to a karaoke lounge. I envisioned that all karaoke would be done U.S. style, in a bar in front of a bunch of strangers, but as I said, Japan does things their own way. They actually have facilities made for nothing but karaoke, with separate rooms based on the size of the group. Did I mention that they also serve beer in the rooms?

About twenty of us loaded internationals piled into a room made for fifteen, and the show began. Here, I'd like to share something from the bottom of my heart: There is nothing funnier than a drunk Japanese guy who barely speaks English and cannot carry a tune in a bucket, trying to sing an American bubblegum pop song. I nearly wet my pants watching them. It was almost as funny as when one of the Americans who traveled with me, a rather stuffy guy known for no antics whatsoever, busted out with his rendition of "Sitting on the Dock of the Bay." His performance was beyond horrible, but I suppose that's kind of the point of karaoke anyway. When it was my turn, of course my performance mode kicked into high gear, and I took those folks to school on how to sing karaoke with a splendid version of "Mustang Sally." Jaws of all nationalities dropped, and the room agreed that mine was the best karaoke performance any of them had ever experienced. That was followed later in the night by "Hard to Handle," "Wonderful Tonight," and an encore duet with the Brit of Sinatra's "I Did It My Way."

Not long after we returned from Japan, I received a very important promotion, and I now manage the largest department at the company. My wife is convinced that my performance that night led to the promotion, especially since I'm now known throughout all the global offices of my company as the American karaoke king!

I Almost Lost My Teeth!

I absolutely hate drunks. They are usually obnoxious and mean, shamelessly invade everyone's personal space, and are always just a real pain in the backside to be around—and that's when they're at their best. At their worst, they drive drunk, placing the entire public at risk. Since most bands make their living playing in bars, nightclubs, private parties, and the like, it simply goes without saying that every band has to contend with the intoxicated. There's just no way around it unless you are a church band or perhaps a classical musician. Drunks heckle and loiter around the sides of the stage, requesting the stupidest songs imaginable. They start fights, hit on your girlfriend (which can also start a fight), and try to make conversation with the band during breaks. This can and will really get on your nerves. They insist on standing way too close for comfort, talk way too loudly, and make absolutely no sense whatsoever. I think all musicians will agree that the most egregious, apprehensible, and disgusting thing a drunk can do is attempt to get onstage to play or sing with the band. Even attempting such a dastardly deed should constitute a butt-kicking. Sorry for the sermon, but I feel better now.

This story comes to me from one of my customers. As I explained, my work allows me to talk to musicians day in and day out, since we provide advice on how to mic particular instruments, the best microphone to use on certain vocals, and what they should do after fiddling with the electronics and letting out the factory-installed smoke. A customer we'll call Matt rang us up to ask for a recommendation for a clip-on microphone to use with his tenor saxophone. I could have easily given a basic answer, based on the frequency response curve of the mic in reference to the capability of a sax, as well as looking at the sound pressure level, but I prefer to spend a little time finding out what the customer really needs. I like to know what kind of music he plays, where he plays, what sound he's after, how much he wants to spend, and what he is using now. I really want to give everyone exactly what they're looking for, so I take the time.

Matt was part of an R&B band horn section that played every weekend and had been using a traditional stand-mounted microphone. He had absolutely no issue with the sound of the mic he was using; in fact, he really liked it.

"Do you move around a lot?" I asked. "Is that why you want a clip-on microphone, so you can dance around a bit?"

"No," he replied. "I'm usually stationary. With four horns in the band, we pretty much stay in one place."

That baffled me a bit, so I asked why he felt the need to switch from something that appeared to work well for him. Matt went on to relay the story of his last gig over the previous weekend, and his request for a clip-on microphone suddenly made sense. As it turned out, Matt had the most unique reason I'd ever heard of for needing a clip-on mic.

As an R&B band, they played in a lot of lively places. In other words, there was always a lot of dancing and partying, coupled with lots and lots of drinking. This isn't always an issue for bands and is, in fact, encouraged in some ways, but on that particular weekend, things were thrown a little out of control. A couple guys got plastered and broke out into a fight right in front of the stage. The stage at the venue was very low, only about twelve inches off the floor, so the fight ended up moving onto the platform. One drunk punched the other, knocking him onto the stage right in front of the horn section. As Matt's bad luck would have it, he slammed right into the sax player's microphone stand and knocked it straight back into the saxophone. That, in turn, slammed into his mouth. "He damn near knocked my front teeth out!" Matt practically yelled into the phone. "The drunken bastard almost ruined my career right there on the spot. There's no way I'm gonna let that happen again, and I figure a clip-on mic could prevent it in the future."

Mat made an excellent point, so I recommended one of our clip-on microphones and updated our knowledge base documentation with what microphone to use to prevent a performer from needing a dentist after the

show.

The Drunk Band at My Wedding

In my opinion, there are only a few unpardonable sins. For those Bible scholars among you, I realize scriptures only refer to one, but I'm taking literary license and adding a couple more. First, never, ever enter into a financial deal of any kind with a friend. I admit that I've committed this sin a couple times, and I've paid the price. The second sin is by far the worst of the two, so bad that committing it should immediately condemn one to hell, without passing go or collecting $200! Perhaps that's a bit harsh, since I'm sad to say I'm guilty of this one as well, so please listen and learn from my mistake: Do not, under any circumstances, ask musicians to be part of your wedding party!

I met my wife about a year after leaving my band, Stonehenge. To say she and I came from different backgrounds would be a huge understatement. I was the longhaired, tequila-guzzling, womanizing lead singer of a rock 'n' roll band. One of my nicknames was Wildman, and that summed it up fairly closely. My bride-to-be, on the other hand, was the picture of innocence, a good Christian girl who was raised on a farm by conservative grandparents, sort of a Shirley Temple meets Elly May. It was safe to say she had never witnessed a circle party, didn't know what a bong was, and believed a shotgun was just something men used to shoot squirrels. Imagine what she thought when she met my musician friends!

When it came to our wedding planning, I didn't get my way. I wanted to hire a singer I knew from a rock band, and I had some great suggestions for tunes, but she wouldn't have it. Instead, we had a female opera singer and a male tenor, and the music was very traditional. About the only choice left to me was that of the groomsmen, and after the fact, I wished she had made that choice as well. Of course I opted for musicians, and that turned out to be quite a mistake.

First, there were major issues getting the guys measured for their tuxedos. It was a fight from the start, and I had to call most of them daily to ask if they'd taken care of it yet. It finally happened, and luckily, I didn't have to pick up the tab for any of them. The next problem was that they had a gig scheduled on the night of our wedding rehearsal, one they couldn't and wouldn't cancel, so we had to rush through, with no time for the traditional rehearsal dinner.

On our actual wedding day, the issues really kicked in. First, a half-hour before the wedding, only the best man had arrived, so he had to seat the guests, since there were no ushers in sight. When the rest did finally show up, they were totally and completely stoned; it was quite obvious that they were

groomsmen under the influence. We planned to borrow the bass player's new

Monte Carlo for our ride to the reception, but the car and bass player didn't

show up till twenty minutes before we said our vows. Not only that, but I was

left to do all the decorating of the vehicle myself. First, of course, I had to

dispose of the beer cans and black mollies strewn all over the seats and floor.

When that was finished, I stepped inside and discovered that the drummer

was wearing brown Hush Puppies with his jet-black tuxedo, and he was so

stoned that all he could do was smile at anyone who asked him anything.

Luckily, my blushing bride was downstairs with her bridesmaids and had no

idea of the chaos going on upstairs.

The wedding began, and I was shocked when everything went

beautifully, except for the brown shoes that stood out like the proverbial sore

thumb. Fortunately, my bride was so beautiful that no one was looking at

Charlie's Hush Puppies.

The final difficulty arose when I found out the guys had another gig

that night and couldn't stay for our reception. Since it was a Baptist reception,

with just punch and cake, it didn't really matter, but I wasn't really happy

about their early departure. On a positive note, the band looked good at that

gig, all decked out in tuxedos, brown Hush Puppies and all!

Jerked out of Bed by a Great Dane

I think most would place this story in the really-hard-to-believe

category. As I've said about other tales in this anthology, let me assure you

that it did happen. What you are about to read is the best retelling as my

drunken memory from the 1970s allowed me to recollect. You'll find several

colorful characters within: our guitar player, Rudy; an extremely hot, bleach-

blonde, Zeppelin-loving daughter of a radio DJ, whom I'll refer to as the

Wisconsin chick; Samantha, aka Sam, a gigantic Great Dane; and, of course,

yours truly.

The Wisconsin chick and Rudy were first cousins, and whenever she

was in town, she came to our band practices and gigs. She was so hot, slim

with long legs, nearly white-blonde hair, gobs of expertly applied makeup, and

ripped-up jeans that left very little frayed denim in all the right places. At first,

I was sure she was my hippie soulmate; I later discovered she was not even

close, but that is a whole other story in itself. Nevertheless, we dated for a

while, and we were quite inseparable. Even when she returned to Wisconsin,

she called often, and we spent forever on the phone, much to the detriment of her father's phone bill. Whenever she returned to town, she stayed with

Aimee, her other cousin and the proud owner of Samantha, a Great Dane.

Sam was huge, the biggest dog I had ever seen. Great Danes are

known for being friendly, but I don't think she ever received that memo,

because she was just plain mean until she got to know a person. Not only

that, but she was also extremely protective and territorial, something to keep

in mind as you continue reading this story. It took Sam forever to get used to

me, and even then, I don't believe she cared for me all that much and merely

tolerated my existence.

One of the scariest moments in my life occurred when I took the

Wisconsin chick home from a date and discovered that she had forgotten her

house key. Since no one was home, I had to do the gentlemanly, heroic thing

and climb in through a second-story window to open the door. I slowly slid

the window open about an inch and softly said, "Nice puppy, Sam. It's just

me, girl. Please don't eat me." It turned out that the dog was locked in

another room and could not get to me, but she was about to have a

conniption, and to be honest, so was I. Isn't it amazing the feats of bravery a

man will perform to impress a woman? I was about to become Purina Dog

Chow and scared out of my drawers, but I still acted like a Navy S.E.A.L. on

a mission to save a damsel in distress.

Another weekend, when the Wisconsin chick was back in her home

state, Aimee and her mom asked Rudy to house- and dog-sit while they took a short trip. Rudy and I decided to take advantage of the situation and spend

the weekend writing some new material, so we bought a boatload of beer,

packed up our guitars, and headed to Aimee's house. Sam was calm enough

and actually ignored us for the most part, so we just went about our business,

working on tunes and slurping beer. Truth be told, we actually did a whole lot

more drinking than writing. I remember writing some lyrics about Samwise

Gamgee from *The Lord of The Rings*, something I am still nuts over. After all,

Led Zeppelin wrote a verse about Gollum in their "The Battle of Evermore,"

so I figured I could do the same for the one I consider the real hero in the

epic tale. To be honest, the lyrics were really awful, so we didn't do anything

with them. Today, I'm actually quite proud of the fact that I was able to

realize and admit that and choose not to pursue it. How many songs have you

heard someone sing or play that caused you to ask, "Man, do they really think

that song is worth being played for other people? What the hell are they

thinking?" Maybe I'm my own worst critic, but I'm sure no one would want

to hear my Samwise song.

　　　After many, many beers, I headed up to the second floor to catch

some sleep. What I did not realize as I fell into the bed was that I had chosen

the very place where Sam usually slept, and she was not happy about it in the

least. She jumped into the bed with me—or actually on top of me since it was

a twin-sized bed—and I proceeded to shove the huge animal back onto the

floor. That brought about a round of growls and barks, followed by her stubbornly jumping back into bed with me. Of course I kicked her out again, then rolled over and buried my face deep in the pillow, the effects of alcohol becoming increasingly evident. The next thing I knew, I was startled by an awful pain in my left shin, and I realized Sam was the culprit; that dog had my leg in her mouth and was pulling on it violently, attempting to jerk me right out of bed. I was drunk, but I wasn't so inebriated that I failed to realize I was about to lose a leg to a real, live bitch. I managed to free my throbbing limb from her jaws, and she immediately jumped back into bed with me, where she stayed the rest of night.

I'm sure you're wondering why I didn't simply move to another bed, but I had far too many beers for that. In my defense, I'm sure I'm not the first musician or the last to get drunk and wake up the next morning in bed with a real dog.

Stepped on His Own Hangy-Down Thing

I have mentioned several times in this book that musicians get very few opportunities to make it. In fact, many very accomplished, well-deserving players get none. It seems the music business is one industry in which the American Dream just doesn't apply. Without regard for skill, no matter how hard a musician tries, he may never succeed. I've known many incredible musicians who gave it their all but could never rise above the local club scene. In my introduction to this book, I referred to local legends, those folks who should be at the top, selling records and making personal appearances before thousands of adoring fans. That is why I always counsel younger players to grab every opportunity with both hands and hang on tight, because they are few and far between. Let me make this crystal clear to all of you: There is no shame in not making the big time, as long as you know you gave it your best shot. On the other hand, there is plenty of shame for those musicians who screw up their chances simply by stepping on their own hangy-down things or because they suffer from a severe case of cranial rectosis! I have no sympathy for you whatsoever. In the words of that famous American, Major Payne, "If you want sympathy, look in the dictionary between shit and syphilis."

In what ways do musicians screw up their opportunities? That's a fair question, and there are many answers. Some just do not recognize it when it appears. For example, some turn down freebies, not realizing that a record company is sending an A&R rep there to look for talent. Some lack confidence and simply let opportunities pass them by because they don't feel good enough. It is an admirable thing to be humble, but letting fear get in the way is inexcusable. Others let other obstacles get in the way, like girlfriends, jobs, or bandmates. Some are just unwilling to do what it takes. In some ways, these reasons may be understandable. Perhaps some are unforgivable, but it is easy to see why musicians sabotage their chances, especially if said musicians are young and inexperienced when the opportunities come knocking. In my opinion, regardless of age, there is one unforgivable, unpardonable excuse for missing out on an opportunity, and that is the pathetic crutch of substance abuse.

Jamie was not just any horn player but an extremely gifted one, often referred to as a prodigy. His amazing natural talent was a double-edged sword, though, something of a problem, because it meant he didn't have to really work at it to be better than everyone else. For that reason, he took his skills for granted and did not appreciate the gift he had. He also had a real drug problem and just could not get that monkey off his back, though it wasn't as if he ever made any concerted effort to do so.

I heard about Jamie from a contact, Michael, in Anaheim, California a few years ago, at a NAMM show. Former band parents have an uncanny gift for sniffing one another out, kind of like one Mason can pick out another one in a crowd. We immediately started swapping band parent stories, and that was when he told me about Jamie, a high school freshman he met while he was serving as a devoted band parent.

Band parents are a special breed of individuals, totally consumed by the desire to see their children succeed. They attend every football game and band competition, even when they know their band has no chance of winning. That convoy of seventy-five decorated minivans will follow those band buses every time as they head out to Friday night football games and Saturday band competitions. They chaperone during overnight trips at remote competitions and put in countless hours at fundraisers. I truly believe that if church members were even half as dedicated as band parents, everyone would be a convert. During my seven years as a band parent, I observed some very good kids passing through the program. Actually, nearly all of them were great, but there were a few I wanted to take out behind the woodshed.

According to Michael, without a doubt, Jamie was the worst behavior problem to ever pass through their band program. He refused to listen to anyone, especially band parents. He was disruptive and disrespectful, and his substance abuse began at a young age. He was also a born leader and held a cult leader-type grip on many other kids. On overnight band trips, they had to station a band parent outside Jamie's room to ensure that he did not break curfew. Nevertheless, on one trip during his senior year, he managed to sneak a freshman girl into his room, while his roommates covered for him.

As bad as Jamie was, there was an even bigger problem: While it was admirable that the band director had made it his mission in life to reach out and help the problem kids, he seemed to think that entailed covering for their bad behavior. Quite often, 150 other kids were left behind while he gave all his attention to the troublemaker. During the previously mentioned encounter with the freshman girl, the Band Parents Association president forced the band leader to call the principal. "You call him or we will," he said, "and it'll be a whole lot better for your career if you make the call."

Every year, the kids and parents looked forward to the senior awards banquet, a common event in most schools. It was always cool to hear what the kids planned to do after high school and to cheer on those who received awards and scholarships. In Jamie's senior year, all looked on in horror as he received award after award from the band director, culminating in a full-ride music scholarship to a very prestigious university. After such horrendous, despicable behavior and being a bad influence, he certainly didn't deserve to be rewarded. Even worse, everyone knew he would just piss away the scholarship, because no college program would tolerate his bad behavior. Everyone was in agreement that the scholarship should have gone to someone who would have appreciated and used it, but what was done was done, and there was nothing anyone could do about it.

So what happened? Did the band director's special attention finally pay off and coerce Jamie into getting his act together? Well, to quote Wayne Campbell, "Sha, right! And monkeys will fly out of my butt!" Jamie did exactly as everyone thought he would. By his second semester, his drug problem was so bad that the school put his scholarship on hold while he went to rehab. After several arrests, they finally took the scholarship away entirely, and he dropped out. The last anyone heard, he's been in and out of jail and no longer picks up his horn.

This story really pissed me off when Michael shared it with me. My own son took on a music career, and I paid for his five years of college out of my own pocket. All the while, this naturally talented brat was given every opportunity under the sun but carelessly chose to throw it all away. I don't know who the real villain is, Jamie or the high school band director, but it was a tragedy all the same.

Saturday Satan, Sunday Saint!

What does it mean to lead worship Sunday, after a Saturday night bar gig? Well, I guess at one time, I was quite the hypocrite. Then again, to some extent, all of us can be considered a bit hypocritical about one thing or another. For example, we may openly blast a politician for cheating on his taxes, yet we don't declare that money we received for mowing a neighbor's yard every week. We may openly criticize disco music but secretly have a Bee Gees CD tucked way down at the bottom of the case and pull it out when we are alone in the car; even more pathetic, we know every word of the lyrics and often envision ourselves in a white leisure suit, tearing up the dance floor. What's all that about letting him who has no sin cast the first stone? Speaking of sin, we usually associate hypocrisy with religious beliefs, and this story is definitely in that vein. Don't worry though: It isn't a sermon, so there is no need to rip these pages out and move on to the next story. Instead, it's the tale of a weird, funny, and somewhat tragic period in my life when I could have most definitely been classified as a hypocrite. On a side note, my wife gets extremely embarrassed when I talk about my drunken, club-playing days of debauchery. I guess I shouldn't share these stories with such a gleam in my eye and such excitement in my voice, but I find it kind of difficult to look down at the floor in shame. After all, as I once heard it said, if sin wasn't fun, nobody would do it.

During my late teens, I was busy with Stonehenge, playing clubs all over Cincinnati. I lived the rocker lifestyle in the 1970s, and of course that included chasing skirts, drinking beer, playing loud music, smoking pot, chasing skirts, drinking tequila, and, of course, chasing skirts. I'm sure many of you lived much the same way back then, if only you could remember it. I had a real problem, though, because I still had very strong religious convictions.

I was born and raised as a strict Southern Baptist and attended services every time the doors were open. If you don't know what it meant to be a Southern Baptist in the seventies, let me fill you in. First, zero, *nada*, absolutely no alcohol consumption was allowed. As a current student of the Bible, I can tell you there is nothing scriptural about this belief, but it was a big part of being a Baptist back then. Second, rock 'n' roll was considered to be a thing of the devil, end of argument. Again, there is nothing scriptural to back that up, but there was no telling any old-line Baptist that. Third, many Baptists seemed to think there was an eleventh commandment, "Thou shalt not dance." Those were the big three beliefs most relevant to this story, although there were several other only slightly minor Baptist thou-shalt-nots as well, such as the forbidding of men from having long hair or wearing blue jeans to church. I won't argue about smoking pot and chasing skirts, as I'd have to plead guilty on those two.

Bearing all those do's and don'ts in mind, I'm sure you can see my dilemma. Nearly everything I did as a musician was disallowed and considered a sin by my church. What was a poor rock 'n' rollin', Southern Baptist boy to do? Did I have to give up one to cling to the other? Could I possibly change 200 years of Baptist beliefs just to fit my needs? Well, in the end, I did what I thought was the most logical thing: I kept my rock 'n' roll life and church life completely separate from one another. In other words, I lived a double-life, and there's that hypocrisy I told you about. Do you feel my pain? Don't worry, for it gets much, much worse.

I did a fairly good job of keeping my two identities secret. All the old ladies at church thought I was the perfect Christian boy, even if they did often mention that I was in very bad need of a haircut. If you asked any of my bandmates or people in the clubs about me, they would have laughed and said, "He sure ain't no saint." Very few people, if any, knew me in both worlds, and if they did, it was only because they were living the same lie I was. I did such a good job of keeping my rock 'n' roll secret from the church that they elected me as the music director, even though I was only 18 years old. If they only knew what they had done! I actually took the role very seriously and did a very good job, but I had one really big problem: Saturday night gigs.

Imagine, for a moment, if you will, my band, the house band at an illegal gambling casino and whorehouse, playing and drinking till two a.m. on a Saturday night. I then drove home, one of those highly stupid things I regret, and crawled into bed around four or so, only to be awakened by Dad's off-key Southern gospel records blasting through the wall at seven thirty in the freaking morning on Sunday. I got up, still stoned, and staggered into the bathroom, nauseated from the smell of bacon frying in the kitchen. I puked, embracing the porcelain altar, then jumped in the tub for an incredibly long shower, all while making all kinds of promises to God about what I would do or not do if He would only release me from the scourge of that headache. Then, off to church I went, hung over beyond belief.

In the Lord's house, I took my place behind the pulpit and humbly said, "Please turn to Page 386 in your hymnals, 'Bringing in the Sheaves.'" I often wonder if I had lingered in that dual identity, what level of hell Dante would have placed me in. I would imagine Circle 8: Malebolge "The Fraudulent" would have been a good fit.

Crossroads Biker Bar

Every musician has a favorite venue, that one special location where you look forward to setting up and jamming. For some, it may be a real classy place, the kind you usually don't play. For others, it's a place with a very large stage, with lots of room to set up and move around. Still others may be jazzed about a cozier, intimate place. Some bands get excited about places with great sound systems; this is understandable, since any hall you don't have to lug your PA into is great. A place with awesome acoustics turns many musicians on and may have them saying, "Man, we always sound great at that place. I don't know what it is, but I love playing there!" Of course there are also those places that seem to always draw a great audience. At these places, the crowd gets fired up easy, and that, in turn, fires the band up. It goes without saying that high-paying gigs are always favorites, high on everyone's list. For many musicians, though, there are places they love to play without any clear reason at all. Maybe you just connect with the crowd, sound good, and like the atmosphere there, even if there is really nothing extraordinary about the place. For me, that place was The Crossroads in rural Indiana.

For starters, The Crossroads was a biker bar, but I don't mean the kind of hangout populated by accountants and lawyers who ride Hondas on the weekends. It was for hog-owners, the big, burly, rough-looking riders of Harley choppers. It was something like the biker bar in *Wild Hogs*, except the customers were a lot nicer, surprisingly so for bikers. I would never have the nerve to refer to any Harley guy as sweet, but they were certainly easy to get along with. Granted, I would never want to piss any of them off, but they didn't go out of their way to cause any trouble.

The building itself was also a hoot, an ancient stone structure, three stories high and painted powder blue. Sweet bikers and a powder-blue bar? Whoa! I'm sure your gaydar is ringing like a freaking fire alarm, but I assure you the patrons of that establishment were as heterosexual as it gets, and I wouldn't have dared to suggest otherwise. That fact was only made clearer by the biker babes who were always hanging off their arms.

Since we had played several biker bars, we knew how to act around bikers. The most important thing was to just be ourselves and not act like posers, as they called them in *Wild Hogs*. One such poser I knew wanted to fit in and look like a biker, so he went to a leather apparel store and asked if they had any assless leather chaps. "We do, sir," the sales clerk replied, "but just so you know, all chaps are assless. Otherwise, they're called pants."

The Crossroads was out in the middle of nowhere, so the big, stone, powder-blue structure stuck out like a sore thumb. Inside, the place didn't really have any distinguishing features, and it certainly wasn't The Ritz. There were wooden floors, a long bar, and a big dance floor, but there was no stage, and it was devoid of any real decorations or a sound system. It was just a bar, as bars go. Visiting bands set up on the floor, in a very large area set aside for us. They paid an okay price for performances but no more than anywhere else.

Really, there was nothing at The Crossroads that I could put my finger on that made the place extraordinary. I think it was a combination of factors. If you put a gun to my head and forced me to give a reason, I guess I would say it was the attitude of the place. The overall personality of the joint was closely aligned with that of our band. For example, we were known to be one of the loudest bands in southwestern Ohio, and The Crossroads was the only club that actually asked us to turn it up. Halfway through our first night playing there, we had to turn the volume down, but that was only because we were bursting our own eardrums. In that bar, bands actually needed their volume controls to go up to eleven.

One other interesting thing about The Crossroads was their love for the blues. As a band, we also adored that genre, and we could have played "Red House" all night, but most clubs wanted only dance tunes. At The Crossroads, they actually requested blues all night long. Don't get me wrong:

They also loved dance tunes and filled the floor whenever we played a good one, but when we broke into the blues, they all just sat back and swayed to our music, happy as hogs to hear it.

One other very strange characteristic of The Crossroads was what happened whenever we took five. Granted, we rarely took breaks, but when we did, the place cleared out, went totally vacant. We went on two such breaks before I figured out what was happening. While we were playing, they jammed right along with us, but when we stepped out for a minute, so did they. In a scuffle of boots, spurs, and leather, all those bikers headed straight out to the parking lot, and I later discovered it was to partake of a certain five-leafed plant. As soon as we struck up the music again, a stream of people came back through the door, as if a Greyhound bus had just dropped off a bunch of senior citizens at a Golden Corral. The only difference was that instead of smelling like Ben Gay, they smelled like nickel bags. As I mentioned in the intro of this book, I do not wish to glamorize drug use; I only mention it here because it was the strangest behavior I've ever seen in all my years of gigging. Sure, there were always the random few tokers who took off to the parking lot now and then, but never before The Crossroads did I see the whole room clear at once. The first time it happened, I was worried that I'd said something to offend them or that I missed the fire alarm at that ear-splitting volume they demanded.

The Things People Say

Unless you've been onstage yourself, you probably have no idea about the crazy things that are said to or asked of musicians. I've been the lead singer of every band I've played in, so I can personally assure you that it is much worse for the guy out front. Without any hesitation, I can also tell you that it's usually not a hot-looking lady wanting to throw her bra up onstage. Every once in a while, that may be the case, but I'm still waiting patiently for that to happen to me.

I purposely placed this story in the "Yes, Alcohol Was Involved" section because, by and large, the most off-the-wall comments, requests, criticisms, and sly remarks are made by those who are heavily under the influence. Maybe you've never heard anyone say, "Help! I'm drunk, and I can't shut up!" but more often than not, it's the truth.

By far, the most common words spewed out to musicians onstage are song titles. You may think requests are quite innocent and not really a problem, but in fact, they really are, on two levels. First, bands usually plan sets long beforehand, based on many factors, including the number of songs they want to play, the amount of time they have, the instrumentation and equipment available, the acoustics of the venue, and so on. Throwing an unsolicited request at a band can really mess up their groove. Second, without fail, people request songs that are just not in alignment with the band's style. They don't require the same instrumentation, don't fit the venue, or are just downright stupid. For example, it's just plain nuts to ask a band with guitars and no keyboard to play Styx's "Sailing Away," because that song is all piano. How about asking a band without a horn section to play a Chicago tune? Stupid again! I beg you to go into a biker bar and ask the blues band to play some Boy George; if you do, yes, they will really want to hurt you. I've already mentioned an old redneck, green-toothed guy who stood offstage at a country gig my bland played, yelling, "Hey, Rickey, play 'Tush'! C'mon! Play 'Tush'!" and that was bad enough. It was because of that constant bombardment of lame requests that I developed a standard line to announce over the PA at the start of every gig: "If you have any requests, please write them on the back of a fifty-dollar bill and slip it in my pocket, and we will give it serious consideration." Believe it or not, I haven't received a single fifty yet.

I distinctly remember a wedding reception I played while I was in high school. In the middle of a song, a big, mean-looking dude walked up to the stage and stood there with his thick arms crossed, looking at me like he thought I'd slept with his wife and wanted to kill me for it. The stare-down really started to freak me out, especially since I had no idea what I or the band could have possibly done to piss the monster off. Whatever it was, he sure looked like he wanted a piece of somebody. As soon as the tune was over, I humbly walked over to him and asked if I could help him. The bruiser looked me straight in the eye and said, "That song you did a while back, 'Johnny B. Goode'... I liked that. Are you gonna play it again?" Without hesitation, I responded, "You bet we are. How many times do you wanna hear it?" Truth be told, we would have gladly played it all night long just to keep him off our backs.

Not long ago, several musician friends and I were asked to play some old rock 'n' roll at an anniversary party, and on the day of the gig, "Misty" was requested for the couple. I had never sung that tune, so I downloaded it and listened to it in the car, hoping I could learn it on the way there. When the time came to play it, an old lady jumped up and stood next to me and began singing along. During the second verse, she stopped singing, turned to look at me, and exclaimed, "I can't sing with you. You don't know what the hell you're doing!" She sure put me in my place for trying to just wing it.

Another exchange that happens quite often is when a drunk tries to get onstage for an uninvited singalong. I allowed this only once before I learned my lesson. We were playing a gig at a VFW hall, and toward the end of the night, an inebriated gentleman started nagging the hell out of us to let him sing. Out of desperation, our guitar player said, "Damn it, just let him do one song, and maybe he'll shut up!" The drunkard climbed up onstage and tried to pull off a Mick Jagger imitation and dropped the best vocal mic we owned. As a result, that mic never worked again. I shot a nasty look at the guitar player and determined that we would never allow guest singers from the audience to be part of our act again.

I could probably tell you about dozens more events like this, but I'm sure I've gotten my point across. If you are onstage, you will have to deal with people, so make like the Boy Scouts and be prepared for anything.

The Cougar at the Firehouse

The most glorious day in a musician's life is the first time he and his child step onstage to jam together. That precious experience will be etched in my mind forever. The pride I felt is beyond explanation. At that moment, the third generation from my family picked up the mantle, prepared to take the music another step forward. I took it beyond my father, and now my son was ready to take it beyond me. I've actually had the pleasure of being onstage with both my oldest son and daughter before, and I hope we will get to jam with my two youngest in the future. My son is a professional musician, as I've mentioned several times since I'm so darn proud of him for it, and we have shared the stage on many occasions, but one gig in particular stands out in my mind.

In previous stories, you read that I played in an R&B/classic rock band with a bunch of old rockers. Most of those guys had played professionally or semiprofessionally for many years but were now just old, married men who loved to get together and jam on occasion. Every once in a while, we played a gig just for the fun of it. Most of the time, it consisted of a local dance at the firehouse, a wedding reception, or a private party. None of them were very serious, since we'd all been there and done that and were just doing it for fun.

When my son was a freshman in high school, he started playing tenor sax for us. It worked out great for him, since one of our horn players was also his private saxophone teacher, and every gig turned into an extra lesson. My son is a very good-looking kid, and I'm not just saying that as a proud father. He is tall and dark, with a head of hair as thick as a horse's mane, something he did not inherit from dear old Dad. He also has a very nice stage presence and can captivate an audience quite well. During one particular gig, though, his good looks became a real issue for him.

We were asked to play the Christmas party at the local firehouse, and it was one of my son's first gigs with us. Of course the audience had no idea of the caliber of musicians onstage, nor did they care. Most were there to drink something far stronger than eggnog. Boy, could those firefighters really put a few away! I had attended high school with many of them and knew they could drink back then, but it appeared they had graduated to the professional level over the years. Thank God there were no fires that evening, because I would have hated to see them even attempt an emergency run. Of course they weren't the only ones putting away the brew that night, because the women at the party also managed to keep up quite nicely. The crowd grew louder, rowdier, and more vulgar as the night progressed. In fact, I'm sure there were some children conceived that evening, quite possibly on the premises.

As we played, a very nice-looking woman in her early 30s stood just offstage, staring at my son with a huge smile on her face. Her inebriation was obvious, and between every song, she walked up to my kid and whispered something. From time to time, she danced in a most provocative way, a performance intended to entrance my boy. The broad really should have considered dancing on the firefighters' pole, as some of her moves were fit for it.

After a while, my son nervously exclaimed, "Dad, this old lady is hitting on me, and I don't know what to do!" As I said, she was only in her early 30s, so I was offended by his reference to an "old lady," but considering the panic he was experiencing and the fact that she was almost twice his age, I let the remark go.

It turned out to be another one of those teachable moments every father and son share, although I doubt many fathers have to teach their sons how to keep an "old" drunk lady from hitting on them. "Son," I said, "you're a musician, so get used to it. Women throw themselves at us all the time. Just don't tell your mother!"

After a while, the woman motioned to me that she wanted to ask me a question. I bent down onstage, and she whispered in my ear, "I understand that's your son playing the saxophone. He sure is hot!" I replied, "Thank you.

He gets his looks from me. Don't you think you should be looking for someone a bit older?" I nearly fell offstage when I heard her reply, "Hell no! If I wanted someone my age, I'd be dancing with my husband. He's standing right over there."

I looked up and, sure enough, a very drunk fireman was staring at us like he wanted to kick my butt or strangle me with the closest hose. I informed his missus that my son was off limits and asked her to kindly step away from the stage before her husband went postal on us. I was surprised when she did as I asked and sauntered straight over to her husband, who proceeded to rip her a new one right there on the dance floor. After going at it for a few minutes, they headed for the exit and did not return.

The next set was uneventful, but I did ask an old high school buddy about the chick who had hit on my son. He started laughing uncontrollably and roared, "Oh, that's Marilynn, Jack's wife. Don't worry about her. She turns into a slut every time she gets drunk at one of our parties, and she always tries pick up some young dude. One of these days, Jack's gonna kick the crap outta her!"

Personnel

Self-Proclaimed Claptons

Old Musicians Never Die; They Just Get Day Jobs

For about 99.99 percent of musicians, it is inevitable that we will one day have to get real jobs. We fight it as long as we can, but we soon realize the wife and kids prefer to eat every day. We reluctantly condemn our guitars to their cases, at least for a while, trade in our ripped jeans and bandanas for dress pants and neckties, and trudge off to corporate America. As for me, I headed for that big soap-maker in Cincinnati and actually did quite well. As my performance evaluations indicated, I "advanced through positions of ever-increasing responsibility," only to finally reach management level. Still, no matter who you are or what you're doing now, the love and thrill of standing in front of a cheering crowd never goes away. If you need proof, just take a look around at all the reunion tours going on now, bands we haven't heard from in decades back on the road again, to the happy shouts of their long-silent fans. If you are a musician, you automatically have a huge ego, and by God, it must be stroked every once in a while. Maybe that's why I make such a good presenter; quite possibly, the act of standing in front of a group of businesspeople, with all eyes on me, even for just a brief moment, provides a bit of flashback to my time onstage. I just hope I don't ever forget where I am and burst into a rendition of "Freebird" at an inappropriate time. The longer one is in the business world and the further from the stage one gets, the more that ego starves. It never dies and just sits back there, desperately waiting for any morsel, screaming, *"Feed me!"* like that greedy plant in *Little Shop of Horrors*. It doesn't help in the least that you are getting older, gaining a gut, and starting to lose hair at a horrendous rate. Those leather pants just don't look like they used to when one is suffering from dickey-do syndrome, when your belly sticks out farther than your dickey do!

I was middle-aged, balding, and slightly overweight, an ex-rocker stuck in the throes of writing a dull computer program in a tiny cubicle when a young, gorgeous, large-breasted babe moved into the office right across the hall from me. I tell you, that girl was a breath of fresh air! The next thing I knew, she was standing at my door, introducing herself and asking me about my life story. She actually appeared to be genuinely interested. Day after day, she stopped by to greet me with her big smile and bubbly personality. She asked questions about my life and seemed very excited to hear my rock 'n' roll stories. The more interest she showed, the thicker I laid it on. After a while, I started to realize that the young thing was actually hitting on me. I was a very happily married man with two great kids, and I had absolutely no intention of reciprocating her advances, but I have to admit that it was exactly what an old rocker's ego needed. She let me know I still had it. It's easy to see why old guys get themselves in trouble with young chicks, because that attention sure felt nice.

Then came the problem: *How do I let this sweet thing down gently?* It was obvious that she was hot for me, but I wouldn't even think about stepping out on my lovely wife. I dug the attention, but at some point, I had to shut it down. I knew she would be devastated, but it had to be done. *But when…and how? I mean, we have to work together, and you know what they say about a woman scorned,* I worried.

As it turned out, the problem resolved itself in a most peculiar way that was actually painful for me. No, my wife didn't find out about the girl and threaten to leave me. No, upper management didn't catch wind of the possible fraternization and threaten to send me packing if I didn't pull the plug. What actually happened was probably more difficult to bear than either of those.

One day, she was standing by my door smiling, all bubbly and hanging on my every word as usual. After a few minutes, she looked at me and said sincerely, "My mom would really like you. You two are about the same age."

Wham! went my ego, the very essence of my manhood hitting the floor. I was crushed. That young thing, the one I assumed was hitting on me, was actually scoping me out for her mother. My ego took a tremendous nosedive, but I recovered pretty quickly: *Hmm... I wonder what her mom looks like. Nah, forget it, bud. You're married!*

Can't Blame God for Giving You that Voice, I Wouldn't Want It Either

I wish someone would explain to me why the vast majority of people

in this world think they can sing, when, in reality, very few can. I'm not

talking about singing in the church choir or the school chorus. I'm talking

about people who truly think they are talented enough that they should cut

record deals and assault thousands of ears in packed auditoriums. I've seen

the bashful, the shy, and the meek of the Earth lose all inhibitions and stand

before a microphone, thinking they have somehow transformed into Britney

Spears or Rod Stewart, except that they sound like Peter Brady going through

the voice change while swallowing sandpaper. Why are they so delusional, so

completely out of touch with reality? Sure, most people wish they had such a

talent, and everyone tries new things once in a while, even when they don't

believe they are truly qualified or gifted in that area and might not have a shot,

but most eventually realize that not everyone is good at everything. For some

reason, this doesn't seem to be so behind the microphone. If you want to lose a lifelong friend, just tell them the bitter truth: "Please step away from the microphone, because you can't and shouldn't sing!"

This is exactly why karaoke is so popular, the legalized exploitation of those suffering from terminal cranial rectosis. People try to strut their stuff onstage, looking out at the crowd as if they're sure a big-time agent is out there to discover them. Truth be told, karaoke is best when the singer makes a total ass of him- or herself, and that happens most of the time.

This phenomenon is also quite evident in church praise teams and choirs, only amplified due to well-meaning folks with the attitude that they are making a joyful noise for the Lord. Compliments are heaped upon anyone who makes such a racket. I guess if enough people tell you that you are good, you'll start to believe it over time, but that doesn't necessarily make it true; I could tell you a thousand times that the sky is purple with pink polka-dots, but that won't make it so.

One band I was in had to deal with one such a victim of constant church pats on the back. It was a four-piece band, blessed with an incredible three-part harmony. Then there was Wally Spicer. He was a very good guitar player and a much better bass player than I was, but that wasn't enough for him. Wally wanted to sing, but his voice was beyond bad. When he stepped behind the mic, I was actually embarrassed for him. The problem was that Wally had grown up in a small, old-time Pentecostal church, and he'd received lots of encouragement from little old ladies about how great his singing voice was; he failed to realize many of them were listening to him through hearing aids or ears that didn't work very well anymore. When Wally joined a very good band with great vocals, the scalded hound wanted to join in. Of course none of us had the balls to tell him how awful he was. Instead, we chose to make excuses as to why he couldn't sing. Sometimes we told him, "Wally, this song only has a three-part harmony, and a fourth part just won't work." We even tried to blame it on the fact that we only had three mics, but he remedied that by going out and buying his own. When we told him there wasn't an extra channel on the board for his microphone, he just plugged it into his guitar amp, a final blow that forced a response from the rest of the band.

When we finally broke the news to Wally that we just didn't want him to sing, he exploded: "God gave me this voice, and I just hafta use it!" In a split second, our drummer grew a pair and, without batting an eye, replied, "I can see why God gave you that voice, Wally. I wouldn't want to keep it either!"

After that, old Wally gave up and didn't attempt to sing with us, but a few years later, we caught him serenading his bride at his wedding. It was all his three bandmates could do to keep from roaring out loud. I've got no proof of it, but I personally believe his singing may have contributed to his divorce a short time later. God help his poor bride who had to hear it in the shower!

Fired from His Own Band

"There just ain't no way to keep a band together," stated the old jazz musician in *That Thing You Do*, and I couldn't agree more. Something always seems to get in the way and drives a wedge between the players. A woman can a kill a band quicker than anything; just ask the remaining Beatles about that. A girlfriend once confessed to me that she intended to get between me and my band because I wasn't paying enough attention to her; of course she became an ex before she got the threat fully out of her mouth. Fights over money distribution are real band killers, too, as well as the infamous creative differences we hear so much about in the media. Just being together with the same group of people for an extended period of time can cause folks to rub each other the wrong way. Add to that the stress of being on the road and living out of a suitcase, and it's no wonder bands are constantly changing personnel.

While all of the above are true, I'm going to step out on a limb here and say that the all-time, number-one reason bands break up is because one individual decides to be the boss and starts trying to call all the shots. These are usually Type-A personalities, people who feel like they just have to be in charge. It could be the guy who buys or owns the majority of the equipment or the person who sets up all the gigs and feels like they have invested the most. More than likely, the wannabe boss will consider himself the talent, the reason everyone comes to see the band. Man, we all hate that guy! Once this self-proclaimed leader emerges, it is not long before the rest of the members form a mutiny. Take a look at the breakup of Creed, if you need an example.

Often, players are just not on the same page. Maybe some band members are more devoted than others, or perhaps they're just able to dedicate more time and effort to the band. This can lead to a lot of resentment between members. Sometimes, certain members want to push the band beyond the original agreement. Other times, members are just there for the party and/or the chicks and beer.

Band breakups are common, and many musicians accept it as normal. They can join or leave a band with ease and harbor no ill feelings toward their former bandmates. For others, a band breakup can be a terrible and possibly devastating experience, even though it is often inevitable. Personally, I think the worst band breakups are those no one expects, the ones you don't see coming. That has only happened to me once, but I have seen it happen many, many other times to other musicians. Those breakups are usually not pretty and tend to hurt or kill friendships.

The most creative, blindsided, kicked-in-the-teeth band breakup I ever heard about happened to a guitar player I know. Craig was actually kicked out of a band he founded as well as led. That was crazy enough, but crazier still was the way it happened. Before you can really understand the how and why, it's important to know a little about Craig's personality. He is an extremely talented singer, songwriter, and guitar player, but he is also one of the most unbelievably anal retentive individuals of all time. I mean this in a good way though.

Craig wrote all of the band music, set up all the gigs, let them use his house for all their practices, and handpicked each and every musician, rightfully so because he wanted things done right. In other words, he wanted everything his way. Craig drove the band very hard. He expected them to be on time and prepared at every practice. During those three or four hours, he was all business, and he didn't tolerate any kidding around. During gigs, he didn't allow the guys to drink or flirt with women, as he expected everyone to be as completely focused on the music as he was. That total commitment paid dividends in the quality of their playing, because they were one of the tightest bands in Cleveland. Even though they were incredibly good and extremely popular, though, all the guys were miserable. It is a well-known fact that musicians must enjoy themselves when they play, but Craig drove them so hard that he took all the fun out of it.

I'm not sure who masterminded the revolt, but it was probably the keyboard player, since they are usually the most devious. Either way, a brilliant plan was conceived to deal with Craig. Most guys would have confronted him or just gotten pissed enough to move on, but these had suffered enough abuse and humiliation to merit a bit of revenge, to get back at their fearless leader in some way. Judgment day would soon be at hand, and it would be perfectly executed, which was amazing considering that a drummer was involved. Craig didn't even see it coming.

One Sunday afternoon during an off week of no gigs, the keyboard player called Craig and advised him that he was going to stop by to pick up his gear because he wanted to give all his stuff a good cleaning. Monday, the drummer stopped in to grab his drums, claiming that he was trading his old set of Ludwigs in on a new double-bass Pearl set. Wednesday was the bass player's turn, and he called Craig at work and said he wanted to pick up his amp that evening because it was losing power and needed to be taken in for tube replacement.

That weekend, Craig started calling his bandmates to set up a practice, but no one seemed to be home. He left messages all over town, but none of those calls were returned. He became quite frantic and just couldn't figure out what was going on, since they all knew they had gigs coming up and needed to practice. Finally, on Wednesday of the following week, he received a call from the keyboardist, advising him that they had endured as

much of his crap as they could stand. Just like that, the band was no more,
and Craig was completely devastated when he realized he had been kicked out
of his own band.

The Gigger

I imagine that most musicians reading this book are or were also members of your road crew. A more accurate statement would probably be that you are or were the road crew. That is the less glamorous side of the music business, the one most folks never see or hear about, much less experience. Let me explain the whole process for the non-musicians out there. This will also be beneficial for those who can't remember the experience because they practiced so-called better living through pharmaceuticals during the late sixties and seventies.

The gig starts at nine p.m. on Friday night, and you get off work at six, so that leaves you three hours to get home, load up, and hopefully shower, though such hygiene was optional for sixties musicians and those from Europe. You get to the gig, set up, and go through your sound checks. Hopefully, your bass player was able to borrow the delivery van from the florist where he works, or else you'll be in deep feces. Each musician sets up his own rig, and if you don't have a sound guy, which you probably don't, you'll have to set up the PA as well. Five to ten minutes before show time, you're absolutely exhausted and sweaty. Your nerves are frayed, and you're all

pissed off because there's some kind of wicked buzzing in the sound system,

but you've got no time left for troubleshooting.

In struts your horn player, looking refreshed, clean, and relaxed in his

perfectly white pants, ready to go. He opens his case, pulls out his horn,

saunters up to the mic you already set up for him, and has the nerve to ask,

"What are you waiting for, guys? Let's jam!" Striking the stage is a similar

experience, although your horn player has to be somewhat more creative in

order to miss out on the fun of breaking down the set. This is usually

accomplished by mixing and mingling with his fans. Then, when no one is

watching, he just disappears.

Now that you understand what usually transpires, let me share a

specific story with you. A few years ago, after moving to Cleveland, I hooked

up with a bunch of old married guys to play a couple gigs. They were a great

bunch, and they'd all played for a living at one time, but they now just did it

for fun and beer. Occasionally, we threw practices together, and we got

together for local gigs every couple months or so but not often enough to

interfere with our family activities or jobs. Those gigs paled in comparison to

the ones we played in the past, but they still supplied us with the music rush

we needed, and they partly satisfied our insatiable desire to be onstage and in

front of a crowd. Non-musicians probably don't understand this need,

although actors and preachers might. I remember looking at the guys one night while we were playing a private party and saying to myself, "Man, these guys have fourteen albums between them, and this crowd doesn't have a clue!" Wherever and whenever we got together, we had a great time, and it gave us a chance to perform, something we all missed.

Let me tell you about Jonas, one of our horn players. Jonas actually still gigged a bit, and while he was a nice guy, he was also a wee bit fond of himself. He had played with several nationally known artists, and he made that known as often as possible. I can't deny that he was an excellent musician, and he provided lead vocals on a couple tunes and had a fairly nice voice. The only problem was that he reminded me of a lounge singer when he introduced songs, and he insisted on telling the same lame-ass jokes at every gig, which quickly got old.

The keyboardist and I owned all the PA equipment, and since we both had penchants toward the anal side, we arranged the stage and sound equipment ourselves. This meant hauling the stuff up the basement steps, loading, unloading, and setting it all up. The rest of the band, sans Jonas, always pitched in. As I outlined above, Jonas always strutted in about ten minutes before the gig, decked out like pimp, with freshly dyed, jet-black hair, all ready to rock. He usually made a few negative comments about the setup before the show, complaints like, "I'm not loud enough in the monitor." I wanted to say, *"Well, if your lazy ass woulda been here during sound check, I wouldn't have had to guess your monitor level,"* but I had to keep the peace and we needed a decent trombone player, so I just let it ride. I have to admit that when the gig began, the horn section was pure magic. Jonas was really, really good, even if his big head was somewhat intolerable.

We almost always closed shows with Mountain's "Mississippi Queen," a real crowd pleaser. As I'm sure you know, there are no horns in that tune, so that was the perfect opportunity for Jonas to make his untimely getaway. He was always out the door and in his car before we made it to the lead guitar solo, escaping any chance of having to help strike the stage and load out. I'm sure you already know who was on the phone the very next afternoon, asking when he should expect his check. Yep, you guessed it! Jonas, the gigger.

Gimme More of Me!

This story is dedicated to all the FOH engineers, especially those who work in a church environment. Talk about a thankless job! You guys literally make the show, yet you seldom get as much as a passing glance from the audience. The sad truth is that you get even less respect from the talent. Don't they realize you're responsible for that signature sound they get all the credit for? In the crooners' and players' defense, I'm sure they have no idea how much different an amplifier sounds if you move a microphone one inch out and to the left. Most talent wouldn't know a compressor from a tongue depressor, but I'm sure they have an opinion about how to set one up. If you ever want to see a deer-in-the-headlights glare, just ask the talent about phantom power. Still, many singers and musicians see you as nothing more than the fader monkey, the one who sits back there mindlessly pushing buttons and turning knobs. I guarantee that those of you who are out on the road with professional musicians get a whole boatload more respect than the guys sitting behind the console during church services every Sunday morning.

First, you work with presumed professionals. Sure, they may have huge egos and act like babies, but at least they have real talent, enough that people are willing to pay to see them. The church guy, on the other hand, often has to deal with mediocre talent at best, those who truly believe themselves to be God's gift to the music world. You road warriors have been trained, have experience, and get paid, while the church guys, more often than not, landed in that chair behind the console because they were willing souls or, in some cases, were drafted in. Most church sound guys would kill for some training, but it is never in the budget, so they are completely self-taught. Despite the lack of experience and formal training, they manage to pull it off week after week. By the way, they are also volunteers, so no money changes hands.

Let's look at some of the skills the church FOH engineer must have. While they are sound engineers, they are also often expected to serve as video techs and set-up crew all rolled into one. They must also be ultimate politicians if they are to receive even the slightest amount of money to buy and maintain the equipment. They have to be crowd pleasers because the blue-hairs ride them constantly about the sound level. I've known church sound guys who formerly ran sound in bars and clubs, and they indicated they would rather work there than in churches because the bar patrons never complained that the music was too loud, that their favorite singer wasn't loud enough, or that they simply didn't like the tunes. In the bars and clubs, folks often even offer to lend a hand to haul equipment. Church folks, on the other hand, are usually in too much of hurry to beat the Methodists to the local buffet after services. I even heard one sound guy say he would much rather operate the console in a bar than a church because he found classier Christians at the bar. Ouch!

Finally, the most important skill the church FOH engineer must possess is that of a psychologist, a necessity in order to deal with the talent. For example, I knew one sound guy who literally had to trick two female vocalists into singing at the proper levels. One of the girls had a throaty, Southern gospel voice, and she loved to be heard, so she sang way too loud. The other half of their duet was a bit shy and backed off the instant she heard herself in the monitors. To get the ladies to sing at the correct levels, he cranked the gospel girl in the monitor but kept her down in the house mix. She assumed she was loud in the house, so she toned it down a bit. He kept the shy girl down in the monitor but hot in the house mix. She had to really sing out in order to hear herself in the monitor, which corrected her level too. Both girls were happy, as there was a good blend of their voices in the house, and he didn't have to tick anyone off by telling them how to sing. You have no idea what kind of psych job the church FOH guy has to pull on the former seventies rocker guitar player who insists on playing out of his Marshal stack. I've seen sound guys make the guitar player turn the amp backward, away from the crowd, just to take the volume down. I won't even discuss the trials he faces in dealing with drummers who insist on playing acoustic drums and either refuse or just don't know how to tone it down. All

I will say about this is that the poor FOH engineer is always blamed when the drums are too loud.

The worst trial any HOW FOH engineer faces is dealing with the praise team singers and their monitor levels. Let me paint a picture for you: Before the praise team arrives, the engineer sets the monitors and tests them himself. Each mic will be the same level in the monitor and plenty loud, with no feedback, so life is good, at least until the praise team arrives. The first singer says, "Gimme more of me in the monitor." Against his better judgment, the engineer obliges, only to hear the fourth singer fuss, "Hey, now I can't hear me in the monitor!" The engineer cranks her up a bit, and the second and third singers nearly break out in tears, complaining, "We can only hear the band! We may as well not even sing." The engineer then gives them a boost and tries to bring the band down a bit, only for the first singer to whine, "What happened? I was fine, but now I'm lost in the mix. All I can hear is the altos!"

The engineer reaches for her aux input, and then it happens. He knew it would, but he hoped beyond hope that he could escape it just this once. That dreaded, awful, ear-piercing, screeching sound, technically referred to as the Larsen effect but better known as audio feedback, kicks in with a vengeance. Everyone grabs their ears and stares at the sound guy as if he has no idea what he's doing. Then they put their hands around the microphone capsule, hoping to stop the feedback, which only makes it worse. All he can do is bring everyone down in the monitor mix, only to begin the process over again. After the third time, he gives up and barks, "That's the best I can do!" The singers are furious, all of them up in arms, but it's time for services to start, so there is no time for confrontation. The rest of the service goes off without a hitch, and since the singers are in just as much of a hurry to beat the buffet herd, no one says another thing. As the engineer packs up—all by himself, of course—he mutters to himself and the good Lord, "Man, I wish I was still running sound at the Dew Drop Inn! "

Stolen Master Tapes

This story must be told, although I've found it a bit difficult to write. First, the main character is quite complex, so it requires quite a bit of explanation to help you understand. He is also still alive, and even though I've not seen him in many years, I want to protect his identity, as this is not exactly a flattering tale. As I mentioned in the introduction, I sometimes take a lot of literary license, and I will make changes here to ensure the protection and privacy of all those involved.

I met Luke Schneider while I lived in Atlanta during what can only be called his two years of somewhat normal behavior. When I talk to others who knew him before or after that time, it seems as if we are talking about at least two different people, if not three. Luke was an accomplished musician who could play several instruments, all of them as well as the others. Guitar, piano, saxophone, and drums were among his best, and he was also a good singer and a phenomenal songwriter. During the two years I knew him, Luke was married, with a great job and a beautiful home. He also appeared to be a very devoted Christian, although many would say that was just a phase or fad for him; I don't like to judge, but I could probably agree with that evaluation.

During his early music career, Luke was a real hell raiser and had a lot of trouble with drugs and alcohol. He used to hang out in the city square in Atlanta, where he did drugs with just about anyone he encountered. His musician friends missed him from time to time and retrieved his sorry, passed-out butt off the square so they could take him home to dry out. On one occasion, he overdosed and damn near died. Around that time, some of his druggie friends claimed they found Jesus, and Luke seemed to go through a real transformation.

As I previously mentioned, there were some strange folks running around during the Jesus movement, and Luke fell in headfirst. By the time I met him, the pendulum had swung back somewhat from the weird side, and he was actually quite normal, even if that is a difficult word to define. He still had some strange ways about him, but he was off the drugs and living what appeared to be a normal life. Even then, he was very unpredictable. For example, he and his wife went missing once, and neither his parents nor friends knew where he was. One of his musician friends stopped by his home and found the doors unlocked, the lights on, and breakfast dishes sitting on the table, but no one was around. A week later, Luke turned up and told everyone he'd been out on a road gig with a band that called him as a last-minute fill-in. It was really quite odd that he just up and left, without even telling anyone.

Luke went through several failed businesses and a bankruptcy. Then, one day, he just packed up the car and left. I heard he headed southwest, to some small town, and he reinvented himself as a tree-hugger who made a living herding goats or something just as crazy. It was as if he threw a dart at a map and ended up in the most godforsaken place, living on a mountain with his furry, four-legged, smelly new friends.

I lost track of Luke for several years. That was back before email, and musicians have never been the letter-writing type. Then one day, out of the blue, Luke turned up in town to work on an album. Even though he was back, he didn't contact very many of his old friends. It appeared that he had penned some very nice music while sitting on that mountaintop herding his goats, and for a while, he toured up and down the West Coast, playing those songs. He even found a studio owner who agreed to produce the album. It was a very nice studio, so nice that I actually patterned my studio design after it. The owner/producer brought in some excellent musicians to play on the album, and he paid the talent and engineers out of his own pocket. Evidently, it was a very nice piece of work, and the owner was sure he would recover his investment. He used the best engineers around, and that, combined with good equipment, great songs, and even better musicians made it a very promising project indeed. Everyone who heard early demos agreed that it was a special body of work.

Meanwhile, though, Luke reverted to his old strange self, and it seemed he couldn't help but screw things up. The infamous creative differences reared their ugly head, causing Luke and the producer to argue over just about everything. Usually, such differences are settled quickly, and everyone gets back to work after the pissing contest is over, but that did not happen in this case. The studio owner had given Luke unlimited access to the studio, so one night, Luke simply walked out with all the master tapes of the session, never to be seen in the area again, thereby completely stiffing the owner/producer who had so much faith in him and his work. I have no idea what Luke was thinking, because there was no way he could take the tapes to another studio to finish the project, not without being found out. Not only did the producer lose out on his total investment in the project, but I think we all lost an opportunity to hear some good music.

A year or so ago, I Googled Luke's name and actually found him in New Mexico, listed as a member of some goat-herding association. I found his email address, and we exchanged a couple messages, but even though I never mentioned anything about the stolen tapes, he simply stopped replying and vanished again.

Since You Obviously Know More About the Music Business than I Do...

I absolutely hate being the so-called talent in the band. In fact, I've always been happiest when I'm the worst player among them. Why? Because when the other guys are more talented, you have to push yourself to keep up. Being stretched makes you grow. When you're the best or most experienced musician in the band, that's almost impossible. For those with overgrown egos, accolades can be nice, but there's still no room for improvement. It can also be a real pain when you have to be a teacher, mentor, business manager, and musician all at the same time. This can work if your bandmates are willing to learn, have not yet developed exaggerated egos of their own, and are willing to listen to you and draw from your experience, but it's not always a pleasant situation.

My current band, the one I'm currently leaving, The Fools, has been this type of experience for me. It's really hard for me to write this since it is so current, and in spite of their name, The Fools really are a great bunch of guys. I consider all of them friends, even though that feeling might not be mutual much longer if they read this. It is difficult to write this without sounding condescending, though, so I'll try to stick to the facts.

I have been performing since I was 5 years old, in venues ranging from small churches to nightclubs, from wedding receptions to stadiums and everything in between. I've played on albums, I'm a trained recording engineer, and I've mixed bands. I've been backstage at national award shows as an audio advisor, and in my current job, I've provided audio consultancy for several thousand clients. Without tooting my own horn, I can also say I am one hell of a good rock/blues singer and a pretty fair bass guitarist. I think it's fair to say I have a good deal of experience in the music field.

I moved to the Indianapolis area a couple years ago. Being the new kid on the block, I wasn't plugged into the music scene. It had been a while since I had played in a band, but I felt an itch to play. I was also a bit desperate for friendship, so I signed up for the Weekend Warriors program at a local music store. I've mentioned it before, but for the sake of a reminder, the program puts together ad hoc bands for six-week sessions, culminating in a twenty-minute set at a local concert hall. It really is a great program and a good way for musicians to meet. The only issue is that one can never be too sure who will be paired together. Weekend Warrior musicians range from guys taking lessons, with little to no band experience, to good players who have been out of the game for a while. I ended up with a couple very good musicians, but they were rookies who'd never played in a band before. The other guy was also a good player, but he hadn't played since high school, and

he's now in his 50s. Still, we went through a couple six-week sessions together

and really hit it off.

Again, I am not trying to sound condescending, but I have to say

those guys were not exactly the caliber of players I was used to jamming with.

The good news is that they were all great guys and were eager to learn. They

wanted nothing more than to start playing out and looked to me and my

experience to help get them going. To say they were dedicated would be an

understatement; they seemed to have an abnormal fixation on the band, and

they refused to miss practice for any reason. Case in point: One guy totaled

his car on the way to a jam session and damn near forced the cop to follow

him to practice to take the accident report.

Once we started looking for gigs, I found that the guys would play

anywhere, from biker bars to strip joints, and they wanted to play every

weekend. They were absolutely obsessed, even possessed, I could almost say.

Having played for years and paid my dues several times, I really wasn't that

excited about doing those kinds of gigs again, but I sucked it up and started

working with them to book a few. I have to be honest: As a band, we weren't

really ready to play the really good gigs, but I couldn't settle the guys down. I

knew there was no way I could keep them in the basement long enough for

us to tighten it up enough to play the really good gigs, so we ended up going

to biker bars and other real hole-in-the-wall places.

Let me summarize our personnel in the band: I worked hard on the vocals and always knew my parts when we brought in a new tune. I have always prided myself on knowing the breaks and changes. Our keyboardist was classically trained, but without music in front of him, he was completely lost. He had to play with charts in plain sight, and he also had a real problem when it came to keeping time. The drummer was quite talented but a bit rusty. At times, he could not remember how to start or end the tunes, and he quite frequently missed the breaks. He was the oldest guy in the band, so I wrote it off to geriatric effect. Our lead guitarist had a lot of talent but didn't start playing until late in life. He had studied theory, and he probably knew music better than all of us. He struggled a bit when it came to naturally feeling the beat though; instead, he had to count off in his head. To his credit, though, I must say that is not uncommon for new players, and he did improve daily. Our rhythm guitarist was one of a kind. He was an executive at a major corporation and had way more money than talent, so he bought the absolute best equipment available. If anyone was going to play a bad chord or miss a break, though, it was him.

I tried to steer the guys toward the kind of tunes that would land us better gigs, as well as slow them down to work on those songs, but they were about to bust a few blood vessels over playing what they wanted to play. Train wrecks were inevitable for that reason, and in the weeks ahead that was exactly what happened. Instead of slowing down on booking gigs for the sake of working on and improving those tunes, they wanted to practice more and play more crappy venues. I was finally forced to make the decision to leave. I simply didn't have the time or energy to continue working with the guys, and besides, The Fools, as they chose to be called, would no longer listen to me anyway. Now, they will have to slow down, work with a new guy, and get their show together. It's funny, because if they would have done that voluntarily, I probably would have continued playing with them, and we would still be doing better gigs. I wish them well and hope we can remain friends, but I am okay with the decision I felt I had to make.

I Think I Got It Covered

Have you ever heard the joke about the two bulls standing on a ridge, overlooking a pasture full of young cows? The young bull says, "Hey, let's run down the hill and have our way with one of those cows!" The older, wiser bull answers, "I have a better idea. Let's *walk* down and have our way with several." I'm sure many of you have heard that, albeit probably in more vulgar, descriptive terms. The obvious moral of the story is that older folks have a wisdom the young should take to heart. My guess is that if this story actually played out, the young bull would pay absolutely no attention to the old bull and would just run down that hill as fast as he could, huffing and puffing till he chased all the cows away, and there would be no humping for either of them. That, my friends, is the nature of the young; you just can't tell them anything! They think they know it all and do whatever they want, when they want, and how they want, no matter how much you warn them about the consequences. Truth be told, even when things go to hell in a handbasket, just as they were warned it would, the young still don't appreciate the wisdom of their elders and often actually resent it.

This joke isn't just a bunch of bull, though, as it really does have a lot to do with musicians. There are thousands of old-timers out there who are ready, willing, and able to share what they know, not only about music but also about the music business. They have actually been there, done that, and they've even bought the t-shirt. Most would love to keep others from falling into the same traps they did. For example, Pete Townshend, of The Who, went on an all-out crusade to inform young people about hearing loss due to loud music. Pete's ears have suffered greatly for his art, and he wants his experience to keep others from suffering the same. Do you think anyone listens to him? One would hope so, but from the godawful blaring still coming from kids' cars and headphones and earbuds these days, it's obvious that many are paying no attention. Is it a youth thing? A musician thing? Maybe it's a bit of both, but youth, cockiness, and stupidity are probably the greatest culprits. Think back to when you were 17. Could anybody tell you anything? What about at 19 or 21? You probably weren't listening either, and the fact is, things haven't changed much since then.

Let me share a story that will exemplify this point. Matthias, that fine young musician, singer, and songwriter I've mentioned a time or two, was in the midst of putting together a new band. He had a very good drummer and guitar player but was badly in need of a bass player. It seemed there was a shortage not only of good bass players but of anyone who even owned a bass. Somewhere, somehow Matthias ran across a young guy, Scott, who played bass in an awful group; they were absolutely pathetic, even by punk band standards. In any case, Matthias and Scott became friends, and Scott soon found himself being invited to a new band.

At the first practice, Matthias learned that Scott knew nothing about the bass, not even what string was what or what note was on any given fret. Matthias's father, Rocco, was a very good bass player and sat in on their practices. It didn't take long for him to volunteer to take Scott under his wing, so he could teach him to play. Scott took to the instruction very quickly, and within a couple months, he was good enough to play out with the band. At that point, Rocco gladly stepped aside.

Six months or so later, the band was asked to play a gig, and several old rock 'n' roll tunes were requested. Up to that point, they'd only played originals, and they were not very familiar with the old classics. Since Rocco was quite familiar with those old hits, he offered to show Scott the bass parts. What Rocco didn't realize was that the boy's confidence had grown, right along with his arrogance and ego. To Rocco's gracious offer, Scott snidely replied, "I think I got it covered." It was rude, even for a kid, especially since he was practicing in Rocco's basement. Scott could have simply said, *"That would be great,"* then let Rocco teach him the licks, but instead, he chose to piss on the guy who had taught him everything he knew. Rocco looked at him, smiled, and calmly said, "Okay, dude. You've just received your last lesson from me. You're on your own!"

Scott's arrogance continued to blossom, and it was not long before the band could no longer deal with him and his enormous head. Great Scott, did that kid have an ego! Needless to say, he eventually got the boot, and he has not played in another band since.

Freddie's Unplugged Mic

There is a problem each and every music director in every type of program faces, a universal, global difficulty, a hurdle no one can bypass. It does not matter if you are a church choir director, the music director for an up-and-coming theatrical group, the conductor of a symphony orchestra, or simply the lead man in a rock 'n' roll band: Everyone deals with this crippling, nagging, pain-in-the-ass issue of inheriting bad talent. I suppose if you are the founder of the program or had the unique opportunity to hire or recruit all the talent yourself, you might escape this problem, but if that's the case, consider yourself very, very lucky. Otherwise, you will be stuck with what someone else slapped together, and that's no picnic. There are primarily three types of issues here.

First, there is the singer who cannot sing a lick but thinks he is God's gift to the musical world. This, by far, is the worst type of talent problem to deal with. This singer has been told for years how great he is, and he likely believes it. Most often, these alleged musicians weasel their way into the program via nepotism, though some do bully their way onstage. Either way, they are fixed in place, so firmly that it would take an act of congress to force them out. The second type of no-talent are the gap-fillers, those who started out just filling a void when the program or group began or those who cleverly eased in when there was an unexpected vacancy. These folks know they are not necessarily the best at their craft, but they have been doing it so long they consider themselves to be permanent fixtures. The final group includes those no-talents who just showed up in the group somehow. No one really understands how or why, yet you are stuck with them all the same.

The big question I'm sure you are asking is, "How do we deal with these people? Do we kick them out?" I've known some real hard asses who have no trouble saying, "You suck! Get out," but most directors are a bit more diplomatic or are uncomfortable just slamming the door on someone. Should you give them ultimatums, demand that they improve or leave? That probably won't happen. Most likely, they are as good as they'll ever be, so there's no chance of improvement. Still, this is one way to avoid looking like a total prick, in that you'll be giving them some semblance of a chance before you kick them to the curb. Should you work with them in the hopes that they will get better? Again, it's highly likely that they are as good as it gets already, so you may only be delaying the inevitable. Should you just ignore them or try to work around them? Frankly, this is the technique that is used the most. For example, if your drummer is not very talented, you may have to simplify or even have them play a percussion instrument versus a full set. You may insist on no solos to keep the bad singer out of the limelight. You may even use another instrument to cover for the bad player, such as having the bass player hang out on the root note while the keyboardist handles the interesting bass parts with his left hand. Although this is what bands do most often, it is probably the worst possible way to handle the problem of lack of talent.

Let me lay a story on you about a group that tried to cover for a bad vocalist. The Almost Ready for Divine Time Players inherited Freddie, as awful a singer as there has ever been. I cannot even exaggerate how bad the guy was. I had no idea how he ended up in the group, yet he was there to stay, because all the guys really liked Freddie and could not bear to break the news to him about how horrible he really was. When they performed, they always set two guys to a mic. Freddie acted like a forward on a basketball team, trying to block out his opponent for a rebound, so his partner didn't have a shot in the dark of getting close to the mic. His mic-hogging got so bad that something had to be done, but instead of dealing with Freddie directly and honestly, they chose to deceive him.

The vocal director told Freddie that they had decided to give him his own microphone, and of course he was thrilled to learn that he would no longer have to share. During sound check, Freddie's microphone was good and hot in the mix, but as soon as the performance started, the FOH engineer muted his mic in the house mix. He was still in the monitor mix, so he assumed his horrendous voice could still be heard by everyone. Freddie was as happy as an off-key lark, completely ignorant of the ruse, and the band did not have to hurt his feelings. In reality, though, he still hurt the band, because it left them short one tenor in the overall mix.

Here is what may very well be the most profound statement you'll ever hear a musician make: A band or vocal group is only as good as its worst member. That said, my suggestion is to deal with the poor performer. The way you go about this really depends on the circumstances. Use kid gloves and be sympathetic if need be, but by all means, deal with it for the sake of the group and the sake of the music. You will also be doing the poor performer a favor by saving him from future embarrassment. Some loudmouth somewhere will inevitably make a comment about his lack of talent, probably at a most inappropriate time, so have a heart and spare him from that by being honest with him now.

Sure, You Can Marry a Whore, but Don't You Dare Play Rock 'n' Roll!

Without a doubt, Avery was the best keyboard player I've ever met, and I don't say that lightly. As a teenager, he could have easily been on the road with any band of any genre. I met him during the short period of time when I lived in Indiana. Every band within fifty miles and even a few beyond that wanted him in their band, and I couldn't blame them. He was exceptionally talented and good-looking and had tons of equipment because his parents were rolling in dough and always bought him the best. Of course, all things being equal, Avery had his negative points too.

First, he was a spoiled rich kid, an only child at that, so he didn't exactly have the best interpersonal skills. Second, he knew he was good and loved to flaunt it. Talking to Avery was like listening to a Barack Obama speech, in that every other sentence started with "I…" Last, his parents were extremely religious and did not want him to play anything but gospel music. They were quite strict about it, and they even went so far as to forbid him from taking any of his equipment out of the house unless it would be used to play Christian music. This even applied to school activities.

The high school Avery attended held an annual variety show to allow students to perform solo acts or in ensembles and to present music, skits, comedy, or just about anything their classmates might consider talent. They didn't allow just anyone to play, and there was a very stringent audition process. Avery was asked to perform a couple secular tunes with a group of very talented young musicians, and his parents had the proverbial shit fit, though they were too pure to ever call it that. The show was a big deal for Avery, and it would have been very embarrassing for him if anyone found out his mommy and daddy would not allow him to play; he knew kids can be cruel, and there was no way he was going to suffer the ridicule of his classmates, so he chose to stand up to his parents. That was not normal for him, because he was really a mama's boy, but he caved in to the peer pressure. After a huge fight, he flew out of the house, saying, "I'm playing the show, and there's no way you can stop me!" His mother replied, "Fine, but you're not using any of your equipment! I paid for it, so I get to say where it will be used!" Avery played the show but had to borrow equipment for practice and the actual gig. Of course his parents did not bother to attend the show; after all, how could they endorse his involvement in such an evil endeavor?

I hooked up with Avery via some acquaintances several years after he graduated high school, and I asked him to jam with me in a newly started rock band. He said yes on the spot, and that actually surprised me. We were only together for a couple weeks before things began to come together. We already had our first gig scheduled, and we were a bit rough around the edges, so we had our work cut out for us. The gig went okay, but Avery quit the band immediately afterward, claiming he just didn't have the time to commit to it. We took him at his word but always suspected that he just felt he was too good to be in our band.

A year later, I ran into Avery at a store and invited him to stop by and hear the band. With a look of utter amazement on his face, he asked, "You guys are still together?" I guess he assumed we would fall apart after he left. He stopped by our next practice, only to be shocked even more by how good we were. A year of two practices a week and occasional gigs, as well as writing our own music, had really paid off. We were really tight, with great tunes, and our three-part harmony was nothing short of astounding.

All of a sudden, Avery wanted to be part of the band again. Our drummer, who was extremely outspoken, told him, "Do you think we're stupid? You left us a year ago because you didn't think we were good enough. Now, after we've worked our butts off for a year to get it right, you think you can just stroll back in? You gotta be outta your mind!"

Avery didn't expect that reaction, because he was so good he'd never been told no, never been turned down or rejected. It was just too much for him to bear, so he left without a word, bowing his head in shame.

I looked at our drummer and laughed. "Hey, brother, that was kinda cold, don't you think?" I asked. "Yeah, it was," he said, "but I only beat you to it by about three seconds!" Of course he was right, but I think I would have been a tad more tactful about it.

Not long after that, Avery started dating, and he soon married a girl who had an awful reputation for being quite loose. I know, because I used to date her as well, though I didn't do so because of that salty reputation. As a matter of fact, I didn't know about it back then. She was a fun girl, but we just didn't hit it off. Knowing both of them, I still don't understand the attraction. To quote Walter Matthau in *Grumpy Old Men*, Avery was always "as straight as grizzly's dick," and she was definitely on the wild side, even if I cannot personally attest to her reputation being true. Dollars to donuts, I bet Avery's mother had no idea about that reputation either.

Traditions, Rituals, and Other Weird Behaviour

I'm quite positive that God loves weird people, because He sure

filled the world with plenty of them. If you don't believe me, stand inside any

Walmart in America and take a good look around. If there's a discount

superstore in Beverly Hills, I'm sure you'll find some greasy-haired rednecks

wandering within it, wearing too-small tank-tops and pajama pants and yelling

curse words at screaming kids with dirty faces in equally filthy diapers. I

personally get a real kick out of watching people, especially weirdoes. I miss

the days when mirrored sunglasses were chic, because I could sit on a bench

and stare at human beings all day without their knowledge behind those

shades—and here you thought we were just watching for babes! Rest assured

that odd ducks are not confined to Walmart and flea markets though. If you

look on any stage in any club or concert hall, I guarantee you'll spot some of

the strangest people on the planet. How can I say that? Because having spent

thirty-five-plus years onstage with literally hundreds of musicians, I'm more than qualified to recognize the weird. One might also say it takes one to know one, but I won't get into that.

You might be wondering what makes musicians so weird. It's a perfectly legitimate question, and I'm happy to share my take on it. First, let me get the obvious out of the way: drugs and alcohol. Yes, years of substance abuse can lead to advanced cases of weirdness. We have all seen examples of this among rock stars, but I've also seen it infect local musicians.

Being on the road too long can also definitely bring about symptoms of weirdness. I know a FOH engineer who developed a minor case of pyromania and started making his own fireworks inside his hotel room during times of extreme boredom. He even set one of his creations off inside a bowl of condiments in a green room at a gig, then ran like hell. Can you imagine what kind of mess an exploding bowl of ketchup and mustard makes? The band manager got a real butt-chewing for it, understandably so.

Another contributor to musician weirdness is the fact that many musicians have never worked a real job. They may live in a basement apartment at their girlfriend's parents' house, sleep all day and jam all night, and are only around other musicians, drunks, stoners, and groupies. Since they do not visit regular jobs, where they would be surrounded by regular co-workers and customers, they have little interaction with normal, regular people, and they develop some very abnormal behavior as a result.

One final contributor to weird musician behavior is the odd traditions they develop. At some point, they may forget why they even do these things, yet they continue simply out of habit. For example, one band I was in performed a certain ritual: We gathered at the bar just moments before going onstage and downed shots of whiskey. I believe the routine started at one of our first gigs, in an effort to settle our nerves, but it soon became a tradition. We once played at a concert hall that did not serve alcohol, so we walked several blocks to find a local bar that would provide our ritual shots; it was such a necessity that we were almost late going on for our set.

Have you ever seen a band rider, that list of things the artists require? These can range from equipment needs to food and drink, and some can be quite ridiculous. For example, Van Halen's rider supposedly requires bowls of M&Ms to be placed in the green room, with all the brown candies removed. Quite often, even the band members can't remember why certain items are on the riders, yet they are still compelled to stick to the traditions of unknown origins.

The strangest tradition I've ever heard about belonged to a drummer named Lynn. He—yes, *he*, in spite of the name—was an extraordinary drummer and actually had some success playing with several big-name performers in Las Vegas. It is my understanding that he stopped getting calls to tour with the big guys because he was too much of whiner, a crybaby. Once you get that kind of reputation in the music business, you're done. You may be able to act that way if you are the headliner, but it won't fly for hired guns. There are just way too many guys in line behind you, and that makes you a bit expendable, so it's best to keep your mouth shut.

Lynn had lots of other issues, many of which I'm sure were the result of being a spoiled rich kid. His strangest tradition, though, was to always go outside the venue just before the show and run around the building. He didn't just jog around a couple laps to loosen up; he sprinted around the perimeter many times and refused to stop till he was completely exhausted. I have no idea how he pulled it off, because playing drums requires a lot of energy, and some gigs last three hours. I never did find out why he did it or what started it, but it was a tradition for him. Maybe it helped him slow things down or better find the groove. The guy was fairly high strung, so perhaps it really was just to calm his nerves. If that was the case, though, he would have done better to use my band's whiskey method, because that would have saved him a whole lot of energy.

He's Not as Dumb as I Thought

This story is really a quick explanation of how I made the jump from bar bands to church bands. Please don't panic, as it's not just a cheap trick on my part to get preachy. Instead, I'm including it to help you understand why some of my stories are from the bars and whorehouses, while others are from church. While writing this, I couldn't help thinking of that line from Cheech and Chong, when they are discussing a Jesus freak who says, "I used to be all messed up on drugs. Now I'm all messed up on the Lord."

By most accounts, Ronnie, my bass player, was a few volts shy of adequate phantom power. Now that I work for a microphone manufacturer, I actually know what that means! Anyway, Ronnie was usually drunk or stoned, which didn't add a whole lot to his intellectual appeal, although on one occasion in April of 1976, he showed incredible insight.

Back in the seventies, I was about as wild and crazy as one could get. My two nicknames were Wildman and The Joint, which I probably don't need to explain. I was the lead singer of Stonehenge, and I wore that persona quite

well. Anyone who saw me onstage thought I made Mick Jagger look like
Lawrence Welk. I was also quite well known for my ability to drink; for me,
beer was as easy as soft drinks, and my hard liquor of choice was tequila. Did
I mention that fathers needed to keep a close eye on their daughters in my
presence, a task most failed at miserably? On a side note, I get a big kick out
of *Dazed and Confused* because that film is set in 1976, which was my era; I can
identify every character with someone I knew, myself included, and I was
definitely the guy handing out beer from the trunk of his car.

During that time, I also became very active with youth groups at
some local churches, when the Jesus movement was coming on strong. I had
always attended church, but it was only a small part of my life. At the time,
rock 'n' roll was the most important thing to me, so much so that I readily
broke up with girlfriends who tried to get between my band and me. I
enjoyed hanging out with the church crowd, but they really pissed me off
when they started interrogating me about being in the rock 'n' roll business, as
if I couldn't possibly do that without denouncing my Christianity. As a matter
of fact, I think now is a good time to explain my philosophy about rock 'n'
roll and Christianity: These can and do coexist. I still rock 'n' roll, and I still
praise God. Actually, I praise God while I rock 'n' roll, but that's a story for
another time.

Now, back to the story. As I continued to attend Christian concerts,
retreats, Bible studies, and so on, I came to believe that there was something

else in life for me, something more than bars and dives. It really was a huge struggle for me. I had given up everything for rock 'n' roll, including school, girlfriends, football, and family. I continued in a double-life for a long time, living a duel and somewhat confusing existence as a Saturday Satan and Sunday saint. After some time, I finally decided to change directions and give God a try.

It was a difficult decision, but it led to an even more difficult chore: informing my band of my upcoming departure. The four of us had been together for more than four years, and we were more than bandmates. In so many ways, we were family. I had no idea what I could say to them or how they would take it, but I decided I had to drop the dime after our next practice, and I did just that.

The lead guitarist, my best friend, freaked out, but Ronnie really shocked me. "I know why you're quitting," the bass player said. "You don't think you can follow God and play in the band at the same time." It really floored me, because I hadn't mentioned my internal struggle to anyone. I really thought they were clueless about my other life in the church, but I guess Ronnie was actually paying attention, and he obviously understood the unspoken struggle I was going through.

I stayed with the guys for about a month, until they identified another singer. I guess the moral of this story is to be careful what you say around a drunk, because he might just sober up, remember, and share what

he's learned during his stupors, even before you're ready to spill it.

The Fiddling Farmer

Contrary to popular opinion, the ultimate goal of a musician is not always to find fame and fortune. As a matter of fact, you don't even have to make a living as a musician. As I mentioned in my introduction, there are many skill levels and many different attitudes among musicians, and there are just as many goals for what one wants to do with their music. Of course there are those who have every intention of climbing to the top of the music business, and these will not be satisfied until they have multiple platinum albums and play in sold-out stadiums all around the world. There are others who just want to make a living playing blues in local clubs or working as studio musicians. Some are called to teach in schools, universities, music stores, or private lessons. I know countless weekend warriors who work nine-to-fives for the man all week but live to play the biker bars and local pubs after the work week is through. Many musicians and vocalists offer up their gifts to God on Sunday mornings in the praise band, choir, or behind the console. Finally, there are those who just want to come home from a hard day's work and sit behind the piano and play and sing to their hearts' content. Each and every one of these is a completely valid and worthy goal. Ultimately, it's up to the musician alone to decide what's right for him or her, to do what makes that musician happy. The only unworthy thing a musician can do is sit on that talent and fail to put it to good use somewhere, in some way. I've run into several of my old musical colleagues from back in the day, and I can only listen in horror when they confess that they haven't picked up an instrument in years. What a waste, and it simply breaks my heart.

Jake is an interesting case study when it comes to musicians. He played purely for his own enjoyment, although as a musician, he was a better fiddler than the vast majority of those in Nashville. He attended many bluegrass festivals around the country and jammed with anyone and everyone he could, so he was quite well known for his abilities. Many groups, both bluegrass and country, asked him to join them on tour, and several producers tried to get Jake to move to Nashville and work as a studio musician, but his answer was always the same: "I'm a farmer. That's what I do for a living. Why in the world would I wanna spoil my music by getting paid for it? That would only make it a job and take all the fun out of it!"

I can personally attest to the fact that Jake had fun with his music. Why? Because he was the father-in-law of my best friend and onetime bandmate, Rudy. I met Jake at Rudy's wedding on the farm, and without hesitation, I can tell you that he was the most gracious host I've ever met. He told everyone, "Make yourselves at home. What's mine is yours!" and it was obvious that he really meant it. I also owned a farm, so I hit it off with him right away. I will never forget the man's joy and the gusto in his voice as he excitedly showed me his sawmill.

Since the vast majority of people attending the wedding were musicians or spouses of musicians, there was no need to hire an official wedding band. Instead, there was just an open stage, just waiting for anyone who felt like playing. Musicians came and went all night, but Jake was a permanent fixture. No matter who was playing or what was being played, he jammed perfectly with them, whether it was rock, blues, country, or bluegrass. It was a bit strange during my set, as I belted out several Black Sabbath tunes. I had never really thought of a fiddle in "Snow Blind" or "War Pigs," but that 70-year-old country farmer found a part and made it work. That, my friends, was talent!

Rudy talked about his father-in-law quite often. He was understandably crazy about the guy and took it very hard when Jake passed away. It's my understanding that Jake played right up until his passing. What was it Ian Anderson of Jethro Tull sang a few years ago? "You're never too old to rock 'n' roll if you are too young to die!" I can't say for sure, but I think they wrote that very line about Jake.

Why Should the Devil Have All the Good Music?

I have shared stories about many genres of music in these pages, from bar bands and garage bands to college ensembles and theater. I have also included several about church musicians. The following tale is dedicated to all the pioneers of Christian rock 'n' roll, particularly to the late Larry Norman, who just passed away a week before I wrote it. Larry was often called the grandfather of Christian rock, and this chapter is named after one of his songs, "Why Should the Devil Have All the Good Music?" one of the first Christian rock songs I heard. During my high school and college years, I lived by the clever lyrics in one of the verses: "They say to cut my hair. They're driving me insane. I grew it out long to make room for my brain!" Christian music would not be where it is today if not for Larry. I would venture to say we would still be singing "Bringing in the Sheaves" if not for folks like him, Petra, and all the other pioneers of Christian rock 'n' roll. By the way, your homework assignment is to find out what the heck a sheave is!

I joined—or actually formed—my first Christian rock 'n' roll band in 1977. That was still quite early in the origins of the Christian rock genre, so I guess you can call me a pioneer, of sorts. Even though I had my encounter with Christ, the epiphany that enticed me to leave the bar bands behind, I was not ready to give up rock 'n' roll, and that created a huge dilemma for me. Most church people at that time thought rock music was of the devil, so there was just no room for it in the Lord's house. They claimed rock 'n' roll had an evil, sensual beat behind it. Their narrow-mindedness on the issue was so extreme that I actually heard one Pentecostal preacher state that a demon was assigned to and went out with every rock 'n' roll album. I swear I'm not making that up!

A Christian drummer friend of mine who toured with a group in the early eighties told me an unbelievable story of a church where he played. His van rolled up in front of the church, and the band started to carry in their equipment, but one of the church deacons blocked their entry and adamantly shouted, "You are *not* bringing those drums into the house of the Lord!" Only after a long discussion with the pastor, a threat that the band would not play without the drums, and a firm reminder that they'd be paid either way, the drums were allowed. Of course the deacon sat on the front row with a scowl on his face all night.

I faced very similar circumstances myself. I was a longhaired, hippie Christian in ragged-out jeans, and it confused a lot of people in the heart of

Kentucky in the 1970s. I went through all kinds of drama as a believer trying to play rock 'n' roll in a Southern Baptist church. Most of my fellow churchgoers knew my heart and saw the so-called good stuff I did. Not only that, but I brought a lot of kids into the church. Nevertheless, the older members of the stuffy congregation just didn't understand how someone who looked like me, dressed like me, and played the music I played could possibly be a Christian. Like the proverbial whore in church, I just stuck out.

Back in those days, Christian coffeehouses were a big deal among the Jesus freaks, as I mentioned before. My band played in a lot of them. They were something like Christian nightclubs, although looking back, I think the folks who attended them were a bit weirder than any modern-day clubbers; truly, those Jesus freaks were definitely out of control. The charismatic movement was underway, but no one really knew what being charismatic meant, so a lot of people got it wrong. I certainly don't mean to poke fun at anyone's beliefs, but as I said, we were young and inexperienced and most often acted on our emotions. People spoke in tongues at the most inappropriate times. Some stood on street corners, loudly preaching hellfire and brimstone. I knew a bunch of guys who drove up and down the interstate on Friday nights, picking up hitchhikers so they could witness to a captive audience. People even claimed things in the name of Jesus. One guitar player I knew even threw his eyeglasses away because he claimed God was going to heal his eyes.

As strange and misguided as all of that was, the activity that always seemed the oddest to me was when people were slain in the Spirit. This phrase was used to describe a period when a person entered a state where they lost all motor control over their body and fell to the floor. Such an event was perceived to be a personal encounter with God's glory and power, and it also happened at the most inappropriate times. Sometimes when I was onstage, I got a kick out of watching people pretend to be slain in the Spirit. Just as they started to go down, I caught them taking quick glances to make sure they wouldn't hit their heads on anything. I mentioned this wisdom from Cheech and Chong a bit ago, but it bears repeating: "I used to be all messed up on drugs. Now I'm all messed up on the Lord."

Even though there was a lot of weirdness going on, folks meant well, and we eventually got it right. Many went on to start some of the modern contemporary churches, and several old rockers are onstage now in those churches, with no more "Bringing in the Sheaves."

The Cymbal Frisbee

Charlie, like most drummers, was definitely out there, completely out of control most of the time and always a huge pain in the butt. He was always late, totally right-brained, and could drop into a zone, into some whole other dimension, even mid-song. Worst of all, he wouldn't stop banging his drums during practice, even while the rest of Stonehenge was working on parts. I might add that all this went on even when he wasn't high. I guess a better way to say it might be that he was a typical rock 'n' roll drummer. I can say this because, firstly, Charlie was my friend, and, secondly, as lead singer/front man, it was my job to keep him on a short leash. I rode the guy harder than a cowboy would ride a girl at Miss Kate's Home for Wayward Girls after a ten-week cattle drive. I had to lie to Charlie about starting times, call him constantly to remind him of gigs or practices, and show up early at his house to get him ready and out the door. I really did feel like his mother, but the hardest part for me was controlling him during practices. It was always a constant scream-fest: "Charlie, quit hitting the drums! Charlie, get back in here! Charlie, wake up and get back into the song! Charlie, Charlie, Charlie!"

Every practice was that way, and babysitting our drummer quickly got old.

During one practice in particular, Charlie was way out of control. We

practiced in our guitar player's finished basement, and our drummer was so

zoned out that night that I had to scream at him quite loudly. I am not really

sure what I said that finally pissed him off, although it might have been when

I called him a "little pimp." I had called him that before, but this time, it

seemed to finally set him off. I was about fifteen feet away from him, across

the room, so without saying a word, he just grabbed his crash cymbal and, in

one smooth motion, threw it at me as if he was hurling a Frisbee. Just in the

nick of time, I saw the thing coming, heading straight for me, at neck level. I

did my best Keanu Reeves imitation and leaned back to let it whiz past me, to

prevent my untimely decapitation. The cymbal slammed into a steel pole, and

a fairly large piece of metal, about the size of a silver dollar, broke off; I kept

that shard in my guitar case as a souvenir for many years.

A few months after I left the band, I ran into the guitar player, and

he told me they never realized how hard I worked to keep Charlie in line.

After my departure, Stonehenge couldn't do anything with him, but I'm pretty

sure they still didn't literally cut his head off like he almost did mine.

Mr. Anal

What characteristic irritates you the most among your bandmates? Be honest here! Is it the guy who is never prepared? We all know that guy. When it's time to work on new material, he hasn't even listened to a cover tune with a critical ear or worked out his part on an original song, so you have to waste precious time teaching the guy his part. Maybe it's the artist, the one with zero common sense. For all his extreme creativity and talent, this guy still can't remember what day you practice on or what time the next gig starts. Many musicians are completely put off by the rock star, the guy we all despise. He's there to impress people with his talent and abilities but is definitely not a team player. The sad thing about him is that he's usually not the most talented person in the band. To hear him tell it, though, the band would fold in a heartbeat if he leaves. What about the critic, the one who tries to call all the shots for everyone? He tells the drummer that he plays too fast, the guitar player that he's too loud, the bass player that he needs to simplify, and the singer that his voice is flat. Of course he's the same guy who gets pissed off in a hurry if you comment about his playing, even though he has no problem capping on your licks. Have you ever played in a band with a guy who would

rather be doing something else? Everything else seems to have a higher

priority: "I'm going fishing. I can't practice tomorrow," or, "No, I can't play

that gig. My sister's gonna be in town that weekend." What about the

proverbial prick, the guy who just brings everyone down, Mr. Negativity? His

motto appears to be: "I'm not happy unless you're not happy." He doesn't

want to play this or that song because he hates this or that band. He doesn't

want to play that gig because the acoustics suck there. What's my point?

Simple: There are all kinds of difficult folks in the music business. Still, if you

work hard enough at it, you can probably find a way to get along with most of

them.

For me, the toughest guy to handle is the one with an extreme anal-

retentive personality. The Funk & Wagnalls dictionary would define this trait

as "those with extreme orderliness, stubbornness, a compulsion for control,

as well as a generalized interest in collecting, possessing, and retaining

objects." Freud indicated that this is due to potty-training, but that goes way

over the head of most drummers, so out of fairness to them, I won't discuss

complex psychology here. I've known some very anal individuals, and they

are honest-to-God pains in the ass, pun absolutely intended. I once worked

with a guy who organized his food in the refrigerator by expiration date. I

always wanted to tell him, *"Dude, if it's got green, fuzzy stuff on it or smells rotten,*

just pitch it!" I'm sure you know someone who harbors this unnerving and annoying trait, but I can tell you from experience that having a Mr. Anal in your band will drive you nuts.

Let me tell you about Jerry, a very good guitar player and songwriter with some decent vocal ability. Without a doubt, Jerry is the most anal-retentive individual on the planet. Anality, if that is even a word, is bad enough when the individual is anal about their own stuff, but it becomes unbearable when they are anal about yours, and that's Jerry in a nutshell. He was in a band with a friend of mine who told me countless horror stories about trying to get along with the guy. Of course I assumed my friend was exaggerating, because I didn't think anyone could be that bad. It turned out that I was wrong, and I would soon find that out firsthand.

The band was taking a short road trip and asked if I would go along and run sound for them. Actually, the real reason they asked me was because I owned a very large van that could accommodate and haul all their gear. I knew something was up when Jerry insisted on loading all the equipment himself. It was my van, and I'd been loading equipment since before he was born, so I obviously knew what I was doing. Nevertheless, I kept quiet about it for two reasons. First, I didn't want to start the trip on a sour note. Second, being the old, experienced guy I am, I know that when someone volunteers for manual labor, it means less work for me. Thus, I was happy to tell him, "Have at it."

The trip up was uneventful, but upon arrival, things quickly wandered into the weird zone. Aside from backing the van up to the dock, Jerry didn't want me to do anything at all. He informed each member where they should set up and insisted on setting up the PA himself, including setting levels and EQ during sound check. It was then that I realized that asking me to run sound was just a ruse, that they really just needed my van.

Of course I was allowed to stand behind the console and play fader monkey to stop any feedback, but that was about it. I had been working with bands for many years and even got a proper "edumacation" at sound engineering school, yet Jerry still didn't trust me to do anything. For the life of me, I could not understand why. It wouldn't have been so bad if the guy knew what he was doing, but he didn't. That led to drastic action on my part in the form of malicious obedience; in other words, I didn't touch a thing. *Hey, if you don't want an expert's help, dude, then you're on your own*, I thought. In such times, my grandfather used to say, "Buddy, if you get burned, you can just sit on the blister." He was truly a wise man, because I could think of a few things I wanted to tell Jerry to sit on.

There were many other shining examples of Jerry's anal tendencies, but I think the most incredible display came while striking the set. I watched in disgusted awe as he actually rifled through a bandmate's gig bag and rewound his guitar cable. Amazingly, he was not even happy with the way a guy took care of his own equipment!

I saw a similar thing happen at an open mic event where I work. Since 75 percent of my company's employees are musicians, we set up a stage for a jam session during a corporate dinner. I was tuning my bass to the keyboard when a guitar player invited me to use his electronic tuner. I declined and replied, "I'm okay tuning with the piano." A few minutes later, I saw him onstage with my bass connected to his tuner, checking my tuning anyway. It's important to note that he did not change the tuning of a single string of my six-string bass. I would really like to get this guy and Jerry together, because if anality is not, in fact, a word, they would be the living proof that it should be added to Webster's…or at least Funk & Wagnalls.

Sax Player Beaten Up in Over-the-Rhine

This story was shared with me by my very good friend, Jack Snow, a

working Cincinnati-area musician in the late 1960s and 1970s and someone

who deserves all the honorable mentions he's gotten in the pages of this

book. For those unfamiliar with Cincinnati, I need to tell you about one

particular neighborhood, Over-the-Rhine, where this story takes place.

Over-the-Rhine was originally settled by German immigrants, as its

name implies. Over time, it became one of the most economically distressed

areas in the United States. The vast majority of people living there were

classified at poverty level, and crime was out of control, mostly due to drugs.

Anyone who dared to drive through it knew to roll up their windows, lock

their doors, and pray earnestly that their car would not break down. If you

were stopped at a traffic light, you looked straight ahead and dared not make

eye contact with anyone on the street. All the storefronts and businesses had

bars or cages on the windows. I don't think cops even cared to drive through

Over-the-Rhine. It was the kind of place where any suburbanite just knew they'd be beat to a pulp if they strayed in too far; it simply had butt-kicking written all over it!

It was that frightening neighborhood that Markie called home. The Lord only knows why he chose the place, although I must admit that he had quite a few screws loose, so that might explain some of it. Markie was one of the best saxophone players I'd ever heard, beyond Los Angeles session-musician good. Again, why he chose to hang out in Cincinnati, playing local bars, was a mystery that only the Lord God almighty knew the answer to. I only met him a couple times, but I knew right away that he was quite strange. In fact, Markie was the quietest, most backward and introverted person I've ever met, and I don't think I ever heard him speak. Whenever the band took a break, he just sat near the stage, looking straight ahead and mumbling to himself. He kind of reminded me of Dustin Hoffman's expertly played Raymond in *Rain Man*. There were only a few select people he would speak to, and even then, it was only out of necessity, to transfer basic information. Whenever a stranger tried to talk to Markie, he just stared, mumbled, and walked away.

Markie didn't have a day job, so his only income came from his music gigs. That might have explained why he lived in Over-the-Rhine, since rental costs there were next to nothing. If a band or a studio wanted to take advantage of Markie's talents in a gig or session, they had to pick him up. That was never a pleasant errand, considering where he lived. Even Jack

Snow, a very big guy, was nervous about it, and he told me he often heard gunshots in the area. It was best not to go alone; there had to be a getaway driver, someone to keep the motor running while the other guy went in to fetch Markie.

I knew a doctor/musician in the area who owned a recording studio. His wife was a jazz singer, and they used Markie quite often, in both their studio and her live gigs. They had played together for many years, and Markie acted remarkably normal around them. Maybe it was because they knew him for such a long time, but I suspect that the good doc was also responsible for putting the steel plate in his head.

I have no idea why crazy people seem immune to the attacks of muggers and hoods. Maybe it's because crazies and lunatics are harder to intimidate, and thugs don't like to work that hard. Maybe it's just because the whackos are too unpredictable. Whatever the reason, Markie's strangeness served him well, and he was usually left alone, albeit not always. Jack mentioned that on a few occasions when he picked Markie up for gigs, he discovered that the poor guy had been physically assaulted, to the point of exhibiting a busted lip every now and then. That always put Markie out of commission for several gigs, until his mouth healed. No matter how often it happened or how strongly Jack and the doc insisted, though, Markie stubbornly stayed in that hellhole of a neighborhood. If for no other reason than the protection of his life and livelihood, it seemed he should have been willing to relocate, but his insistence on staying there was just one more thing to add to the list of Markie's strange behaviors.

Influences: Son of a Son of a Player

It's gut check time, kids! Think really hard about this question and be completely honest with yourself: Why are you a musician? In other words, what influences led you to a life of smoke-filled barrooms at two in the morning? Was there a defining event or moment? Did you have a road-to-Damascus experience? On a side note, if you don't know what that is, you seriously need to read your Bible more. I've heard many musicians describe the experiences that led them to music, moments that forever changed their lives. For many, it was watching The Beatles on *The Ed Sullivan Show* on February 9, 1964, complete with young girls fainting and screaming all across America. For others, it came from late-night Southern radio stations playing the blues. How many album jackets and interviews give credit to Robert Johnson as the greatest influence to artists? Many more mention listening to WSM's Grand Ole Opry. I've heard countless stories of those who started out singing in the church choir. For some, the allure of the rock 'n' roll lifestyle screamed their name; they just wanted to be cool and pick up chicks. Some are just too lazy to work a real job. I think Dire Straits nailed it when they sang, "That ain't workin'! That's the way you do it, money for nothin' and chicks for free." I doubt very seriously that any guidance counsellor has ever sat down with a high school student to logically map out a rock 'n' roll career, because there is nothing logical or reasonable about it. Maybe classical music or even music education is advised, but never would an educator with any clout even suggest the pursuit of rock 'n' roll. "What!? Are you nuts? There's no future in rock 'n' roll. Build a bridge, dig a ditch, or rob banks. Anything but rock 'n' roll!" would be more like it. Then they'd probably tell you to cut your hair and shave your mustache too.

For a small number of us, music is just in our blood. The desire and ability to play has been passed down from our parents or even our grandparents. Among the list of musical families are The Nelsons, Abe Laborial Jr., Ben Taylor (James Taylor and Carly Simon), Hank Williams Jr. and now Hank Williams III, Jason Bonham, Miley Cyrus, and many, many more. What is it that causes a child to want to continue in their parents' dance steps? Is it genetic? Is it learned behaviour? Were the kids pushed into it? Did they even have a choice? I have absolutely no idea. We will have to leave the why up to psychologists, but I do know a large number of musicians' kids do tend to go down the same paths their parents travelled.

In my case, my father was a singer and rhythm guitarist. By far, my most treasured possession is his vintage 1970s Gibson J45 deluxe. That guitar probably accompanied him in the million gospel songs he crooned in our family room or at church. Please excuse me while I wipe a tear from my eye; I can still see him, too sick to hardly sit up, playing and singing those old gospel hymns. Dad was a fair guitar player, but best of all, he had a great voice and always invited bluegrass pickers or quartets over at our house to join him. Jam sessions were constant in our home, so it was only natural that I eventually joined in. My brother also played guitar and bass. As I mentioned earlier, I was around 7 or 8 when Dad started taking me to church gigs and stood me onstage to sing. Folks expected some squeaky, pitchy rendition of "Jesus Loves Me," but instead, they heard me belt out some real tunes. Not to sound too arrogant, but I could really sing, even at a very early age.

My brother, eleven years older than me and in the armed services, brought home a bass guitar while he was on leave. When he went back to the base, he told me not to touch it, but by the time he returned, I was a full-fledged bass player. It has always been my main instrument, my passion. By the time I was around 12, I had already joined my first rock 'n' roll band. Dad hated the genre entirely, but he loved his kids dearly and never missed an opportunity to hear me play.

Fast-forward several years, and I now have kids of my own. It was inevitable that at least one of them would become a musician. Actually, both of my grown offspring are fine musicians, and only time will tell when it comes to the two little ones. Talented as she is, my oldest daughter chose not to pursue music as a career. My son, on the other hand, would rather play than breathe, so he is a dedicated career musician. At first, it didn't appear that he was headed down that path. We had to drag him, kicking and screaming, to band in the sixth grade, and that only worked when we made a deal with him that he could drop out after one year if he didn't like it, which he assured us he wouldn't. Much to our surprise and his, he immediately fell in love with band, and over the course of the next several years, he became one of the finest tenor sax players around. I loved watching him play in the jazz ensemble in college.

Here, I must inject another editorial. If you want to hear some great music for free, check with your local university Music Department. It is a real shame that so few people attend the free concerts put on by these young talents. Please support these fine up-and-comers in your community, because some of them are going to go on to do great things in music!

Back to my story: My son always begged me to show him how to play guitar, but I refused. Why? Because I knew that the moment he took that guitar in his hands, he would forever bid farewell to his saxophone. I knew because that happened to me. As soon as I picked up a guitar, I turned my back on the bass. The bass was my natural instrument, but I loved the guitar. After several years, I returned to my first love, and I regretted all the years we were apart. I was afraid the same thing would happen to my son, and I didn't want him to have similar regrets. It wasn't long, though, before a friend tempted him by teaching him a few chords, and the inevitable happened. He took to guitar with a passion, and it turned out that he is every bit as good on guitar as he is on sax, if not better. Now, he is very accomplished on several instruments, as well as a great singer/songwriter. There is no one with a better stage presence, and that's not just a proud papa speaking!

As I think back to my father and my career, then forward to my son, I realize that I took music beyond my father, and my son is now taking it way beyond me. Now I wonder if there will be a son of a son of a son of a player, and I certainly hope there is.

Send That Guy to Diversity Training

If you will indulge me for just a moment, I would like to pat myself on the back for something. Since no one else will provide the accolades I so richly deserve, I'll just give myself some high praise here. I really do know how to quit a band much better than anyone else, period. I've shared stories about those who leave bands poorly, so I won't get into that again. As I've mentioned, for me personally, it has always been my *modus operandi* to leave bands on very good terms. It just makes sense, for many reasons. Even if I have a real beef with my bandmates, I do my best to downplay it or even make up a less painful, justifiable reason for leaving. I'm not afraid to face them, nor do I have issues with conflict. It is just that I choose to leave on good, amicable terms. This attitude has served me very well over the years, and I've even been able to call upon guys from old bands to fill in for me when I'm in a pinch. I've received some great gig leads as well. Not only is leaving amicably the right thing to do from a human standpoint, to salvage relationships, but it also makes good business sense.

Many years ago, I left a band for which I handled all the lead vocals. We had an enormous song list, around eighty-five tunes, and I had committed all the lyrics to memory. I always try to do that, because I hate it when band members, lead singers in particular, must rely on charts. In my opinion, that just looks sloppy and unprofessional, like an actor holding his cue card in camera view in case he forgets his lines. The older I get, the harder it is for me to memorize, but I give it my most valiant effort.

Anyway, I felt really bad for whoever the band hired to take my place, because that person would have to learn all eighty-five songs. That was long before the invention of the internet, so one could not simply Google the lyrics and find them on a half-dozen websites. Back then, I had to sit next to the stereo with pen in hand and write every word down as the songs played. Since it was rock 'n' roll, I had to replay certain lines over and over again, in an attempt to understand what the heck they were singing. Instead of leaving my poor replacement to fend for himself, I wrote out the lyrics for all eighty-five tunes. Am I a nice guy or what?

The replacement they hired was an interesting person. It goes without saying that he was nowhere near the vocalist I was, but he did okay. Now that I think about it, I was much better-looking, too, but there's no need to get into that. Jason had a nice voice, but he lacked my natural edge. Needless to say, the band had to change their style of music when he joined. That's neither bad nor good, but it does reflect on why the band starting learning tunes that were a better fit for his voice. With me at the mic, we did the really hard stuff, as well as bluesy tunes, but with Jason, they leaned more toward the Doobie Brothers and The Eagles. One other very important piece of information you should tuck under your hat is that there was a distinct

lifestyle difference. We were all small-town, country boys, but Jason had spent

his entire life in the inner city. Remember this as the story unfolds.

My departure set the band back a bit, but it wasn't long before Jason

was ready to go, and they started gigging again. As I mentioned, Jason took

them in a different direction musically, but they also began to play in different

locations. Up until that point, the band had played a lot of country bars,

clubs, and quite a few redneck beer joints and dance halls. There's no delicate

way to say this, but they played almost exclusively for Caucasian audiences. It

had nothing to do with racial bigotry; it was based on location and the genre

of music they played. Since Jason had spent his life and career in the inner

city, he started setting up gigs at clubs where different kinds of crowds

gathered. I met up with some of the guys one night, and they related to me

this story about their introduction to a racially diverse audience.

There was a public radio station in town that offered programming

ranging from fire-and-brimstone preachers to *The Gay and Lesbian Hour.*

Anything anyone could imagine could be turned into a radio show and land a

weekly slot on that station, and some really crazy stuff echoed out of those

airwaves. Late on Saturday nights, they aired a music program, and local

bands were invited to set up in the studio to play a set. Jason booked them

for a slot, and the guys in the band, having never been on live public radio,

were pretty pumped about it.

The studio was deep in the inner city, and they arrived around eleven thirty p.m., ready to go on at one. It was a really bad part of town, infamous for gang violence and crime in general. To say the least, they were a bit nervous as they unloaded their gear onto the sidewalk, while bums and hookers looked on. They quickly carried everything inside, only to find the place bustling with activity and tons of people lining the walls of the hall. It also became quite evident that they were the only white guys in the building. There's nothing more pathetic than a redneck white guy trying to act like it's no big deal when he is in the minority for a change. Those guys certainly weren't racists or bigots, but they were just not used to being around blacks and didn't quite know how to act. All they really had to do was act normal, like they would around anyone else, but at that time, they felt that was easier said than done.

Jason was the last to enter the building. He walked in confidently and stood in the middle of the foyer, turning in a circle and looking at all the people standing around, then blurted, "What the hell are all these black bastards doing in here?" The band just about died on the spot, and the bass player immediately started for the door, as his life flashed before his eyes.

Several of the black men stormed over to my replacement, and one said, "Jason, what the hell are *you* doing here? Are you jamming with these honkies now?" At that moment, it became clear that Jason actually knew everyone in the room; in fact, that was how he got the gig in the first place.

Needless to say, that redneck drummer, guitar player, and bass player needed to change their shorts right about then.

Studio Biker Band

As a reminder of a little backstory here, I took advantage of a

corporate buyout and retired very early from that great soap-maker in

Cincinnati. As part of that buyout, I received money to invest in training for

another career. Since I was a musician with a very strong interest in recording,

I used the money to pay for tuition at sound engineering school. After much

research, I found one in an odd location, out in the Ohio cornfields. The

multimillion-dollar facility, complete with several studios, was situated in the

middle of nowhere, but it was actually perfect; with nothing else to do but

stare at the amber waves of grain, we could focus completely on our training.

The school did not operate in the ordinary classroom style, like most

universities. As I mentioned before, it was something like a boot camp. There

were around 120 students living on campus, in little cabins just a half-step

above what we experienced as kids at summer church camp. Mine was

furnished with four plywood bunk beds, a hotplate, a microwave, a small

fridge, and a bathroom so tiny I couldn't even turn around in it. Classes went on nearly around the clock. We sat in lectures all day, then sat behind a

console, recording bands through most of the night. Each session lasted eight

weeks. While this might sound like a grueling experience, I found it to be one

of the greatest in my life. We learned about microphones and mic placement,

as well as external gear like preamps, compressors, and the like. We used

analog consoles, two-inch tape, digital consoles, hard drive recorders, and

recording software. We learned mixing techniques, mastering, equipment

repair, audio for video, and much, much more. My head was so full of

information that I had to forget stuff I already knew to make room for the

new stuff! Several high-profile graduates of that school have worked on vast

arrays of music and video projects, and of course the knowledge I gained led

me to that great microphone manufacturer near Cleveland. It was also a

contributing factor to me opening my own recording studio, but we won't

discuss that under any circumstances, even threats of waterboarding. All I will

say is that if you go that route, make sure to get your money first, before

recording one single note. After all, you are dealing with broke, deadbeat

musicians. Enough said.

The program divided us into teams of six, and I can proudly say mine

graduated with the highest GPA of any team that ever passed through the

program. Of course we had some advantages, as the average age of our team

members was probably fifteen years older than the others, and we were all

seasoned musicians.

As I mentioned, most evenings were spent tracking bands; for me, that was the highlight of the program. Each tracking session was led by one of the school engineers who also arranged for the band. It was a great deal for bands, because they scored free studio time in a nice place with a real engineer. The only kicker was that they had to remember they were there for the students. That meant they might pull an all-nighter and only end up with one tune on tape or disk, because the engineer had to take time to teach us. Many bands recorded entire albums there, even if it sometimes took several months to get all the tracks recorded.

Typically, two teams worked together during each session. The first set mics, while the second actually tracked the band. During one particular session, my team was all set to track a band, and we arrived at the studio at ten p.m., ready to start. We were met at the door by the other team, who was almost at a dead run, trying to flee the building. After questioning one of the guys, we discovered that those kids were scared to death of the biker band they were dealing with. I understood, because the guys in the band were quite scary-looking. On the drummer's belt was a wicked weapon that looked like a cross between a Bowie knife and a machete. The rest of the band donned more leather and chains than you'd see in an S&M porno, adorned with more skulls and crossbones than you'd find in a poison factory.

Nevertheless, we immediately hit it off with that band. In spite of their rough appearance, the guys were really nice, laidback folks. In my previous life, I'd played in a lot of biker bars, so I knew what to expect, as did some of my teammates. Of course I wouldn't have dared to cross any of the band members, even if I was holding an Uzi in my hand; actually, an Uzi might have just pissed them off, but they were there to record, not to kick ass. The kids on the team before us couldn't even set the mics, so we did that as well as track. Once the session started, the guys played some straight blues rock, and they were really good. In fact, the session went so well that we actually laid tracks for four tunes that night.

As the sun came up the next morning, the other team sneaked in to see if we were still alive, but one look at the drummer's knife sent them running back out the door.

Duct Tape Drummer

Drummers are an odd lot. That's probably all I need to say, as most of you understand exactly what I mean. After all, there are probably twenty times more stupid drummer jokes circulating than there are stupid bass player jokes. For example: How do you know a drummer's at your door? The knock keeps speeding up! Everyone loves to beat up on drummers, and it's honestly kind of hard to feel sorry for them. As a matter of fact, the vast majority of them deserve it. Case in point: If anyone is going to be late for a gig, it will be the drummer, even though he has more junk to set up than anyone else. Also, if you've ever tried to tune up or work on a chord progression while the drummer is sitting on his throne, you know it's impossible, because he most simply cannot help beating on the drums while everyone else is trying to do their thing. That gets on my nerves like you cannot believe! Nine times out of ten, the joke about the knock speeding up is more fact than fiction. Don't get me wrong: Some of my best friends are drummers, and these oddities do not apply to all of them. For example, my friend Jack Snow is about the best drummer I've ever known, and no one can keep the tempo like him. He is also the most reliable guy on the planet, but he generally stands alone among drummers. Jack also has a tremendous touch when he plays. The thing I admire most about him is his ability to play with the same intensity all the time, whether in a tiny church or a stadium, and I've played in both with him. That, my friend, is the mark of a really talented drummer.

On the opposite end of the talent scale is Terry Adams, a new guy at a church I attended in Indianapolis. Terry begged to be part of the band, but it was not an ordinary church group. Yes, we played all the contemporary Christian tunes of the day, but the musicians in the band were also members of my R&B band that occasionally gigged on the weekends. Needless to say, we were really tight, especially on the Sundays after we played our weekend gigs. Before I describe Terry's talent or lack thereof, I'd like to talk about him as a person.

Terry was a freshman English teacher at a small school, not very popular with most of his students. He was not very nice to them, and he graded with a tough hand, always making it clear that it was his way or the highway. Since he seemed to have forgotten what it was like to be a kid in school, most of his underlings absolutely hated him. He expected them to act like mature adults and did not understand why they wouldn't cooperate. It was odd that he didn't get along with kids, since he had plenty of his own.

Terry's wife was very sweet but naïve, and the two of them kept cranking out kids, one every year, so many that I eventually lost track.

Terry had played drums in an eighties hair band, and because he so desperately wanted to join our church band, we let him sit in a couple times. We quickly discovered that he was really not all that good; actually, that's too kind, because Terry was downright awful. His lack of skill wasn't the worst part, but I'll get to that in a minute.

The band suddenly had a real problem on our hands. We did not mind folks sitting in or filling in, as long as they had some ability, but the pastor stepped in and all but demanded that we give Terry an opportunity to play. I really hate when pastors do that. I never tell them what to preach, so I wish they wouldn't muck around with band personnel, but that's a story for another book.

Anyway, as I already mentioned, Terry was a former eighties hair band drummer. He basically knew only one beat, and he played that beat incredibly loudly, deafeningly so. He was intense when he played, and he always had this look in his eyes like he hated his drum and was going to make it pay. Every time he struck the snare, he gritted his teeth, and the veins in his forehead and forearms popped out like he was swinging a heavy sledgehammer. Each whack sent a soundwave through the air like a tsunami through shallow water, resulting in sharp pain in the head, like that of an ice pick being jabbed right through our skulls.

In an effort to honor our pastor's wishes, we really tried to work with Terry, but it just wasn't going to happen. We urged and finally demanded that he dial it back before he could play onstage with us. Since he could not or would not cut back on the intensity, he decided to dull the sound by putting duct tape on the drumheads. By the time he got it down to a reasonable level, there must have been a half-inch layer of tape on those heads. Of course the tone sounded awful because of the tape, nothing at all like drums; it was more of a loud thumping, like some old woman beating a carpet in a black and white flick. To make matters worse, when a real drummer sat on the throne, it took twenty minutes for him to remove the tape, and the residue was a sticky mess all over the heads, which certainly made no one happy.

I don't know how the church and the band handled the problem or if Terry ever learned to play, because I took an out-of-town job and moved away. I did hear that Terry is no longer at that church. By way of editorial comment, I firmly believe you can glorify God with any type of music, although I now wonder if eighties hair band music is pushing it. I could be wrong, though, because Stryper seemed to do okay.

The Road

I Hope You Guys Don't Mind Sleeping in the Garage

Wayward Son's Road Nightmare

One of the coolest, most lusted-after experiences for any upstart band is the opportunity to head out on the road. This rare gem of a chance means you are on your way, both figuratively and literally. Just think about it: heading out on the open road, like all the major bands! You've worked hard, and now you'll be pissing in the same trough as the big boys. Imagine rolling into to town with your name on the side of the truck, on the billboard, and on all those posters announcing your arrival. Envision people you don't know paying good money to see you and your band. Close your eyes and think about spending your daylight hours by the pool and your evenings onstage, with adoring fans screaming for more. Now that you've got a good handle on that fantasy, are you ready for the real road stories? Not to rely too much on movie one-liners, but as Jack Nicholson so expertly yelled, I'd venture to say, "You can't handle the truth!" On a side note, I own close to a thousand DVDs, and I'm constantly quoting flick lines, something you've probably noticed by now. If it drives you nuts, you're not alone; the guys I work with hate it too.

As for the reality of the road, what it's really like for the regular guys trying to catch a break, things might be a whole lot different than your dreams of fortune and glory. It is quite exciting and fairly cool the first couple times you fire up the van and head out, but most road warriors will tell you it ain't all it's cracked up to be. Unless you are playing at a hotel, you will more than likely end up in a cheap motel. Even if you do get invited to play in a hotel bar, I guarantee you won't be booked in the penthouse suite. In fact, unless you happen to catch a multi-night gig, you will probably finish up at two in the morning, load up the van, and drive all night to the next gig in another town. If you are married or have kids, you will miss your loved ones terribly. As you sit around in the fleabag motel room or backstage, you will be bored to death waiting for the show to start. You will get sick of pizza and Big Macs, and sooner or later, you'll realize that you'd kill for just one piece of your mom's fried chicken. You'll even get sick of being with your bandmates all the time.

You will also start to develop weird ways of dealing with said boredom. I mentioned before that I knew a sound guy who was a bit of a pyromaniac and started building his own firecrackers, some of them actually small bombs. That night I told you about in that green room, he and the bass player filled a large metal bowl with condiments and set off one of his homemade bombs. The band manager was pretty pissed about the butt-chewing he got from the establishment, but really, it was all a result of boredom.

Quite often, a band finds that the gig and the promised accommodations don't exactly live up to expectations. Case in point: I was quite familiar with the guys in a band called Wayward Son. We shared the stage with them on several occasions back in the mid-seventies, and they were a great bunch of guys, very tight musically. My band broke up, but Wayward Son continued playing and made several albums and a couple videos in the early eighties. I ran into them one night in a Dutch Pantry restaurant, and they were just getting back from their first road trip and shared the following horror story.

Wayward Son was a Christian rock band. They were contacted by a youth pastor in Atlanta about playing at a youth conference. That was a very exciting prospect for an Ohio band that had only played local coffeehouses and concerts for nearly two years, so they jumped at the chance. The youth conference was supposed to bring in several hundred kids, and the band was to receive a percentage of the registration fee the kids paid to be there. The church also promised to provide meals and lodging for the band. All sounded good, so Wayward Son gassed up the van and headed south. Like any band would, they enthusiastically hit the road, eager to take their message and their music to other parts of the country

Wayward Son, like most bands, had very little money between them. To make matters worse, Christian bands did a lot of free gigs, and when they were paid, it wasn't much at all. That said, they had barely enough financial resources to make it to Atlanta. They hit town late Friday morning for the Friday night and Saturday morning conference and drove straight to the church. It seemed to be a nice place, so they had no worries. They were a bit disappointed when the youth director informed them that they had received only about forty advanced registrations, but he assured them that they still expected a huge crowd at the door that night.

Wayward Son set up for the show, and the youth pastor ordered a pizza. As show time approached, sure enough, additional people showed up at the door, exactly eleven kids, for a total audience of fifty-one. At $5 per attendee, the event generated a grand total of $255 to cover the speaker's fee, catering, and, of course, the band. Nevertheless, Wayward Son was gracious, as always, and they played the gig to the best of their ability, just as they would have for a sold-out stadium.

After the gig, they were disappointed once again to discover that the promised accommodations consisted of nothing more than cots in the church basement. To add insult to injury, the youth director had overspent his budget and could not pay the band any portion of what he had promised. He expected the turnout to be at least ten times what it was, so he was at a loss as to what to do. The best he could offer was to pass the hat at the next day's conference; from that, he gleaned a whopping $31.63, since the inner-city kids

who showed up had little cash to give.

Of course the band knew the youth director didn't intentionally scam

them; he was just not a very good event coordinator. They kindly slept on the

cots until Monday morning, when the bass player's parents wired some

money to the local Western Union office, enough to get them home from

their fateful road trip.

Now, are you still jazzed about hitting the road with your band? If so,

let me know, and I'll give you the phone number of a youth director I know

in Atlanta.

You Signed Me Up for What? That's Not Cool, Bro!

As that last story should have taught you, being on the road is not always as cool as you expect it to be. Your first road trip might be exciting, but after a while, things can get exceptionally boring. There is nothing more dangerous than a bunch of musicians and road crew who are bored senseless, with way too much time on their hands. This leads me to a great story I heard from an up-and-coming band just starting to tour, actually opening for a couple somewhat well-known bands. They shared this with me over lunch, and I almost busted a gut laughing.

Marty was hired as part of the road crew. I think he was an out-of-work boyfriend of the cousin of the manager. The band usually just traveled with their sound guy and manager, but new to the road and without a lot of cash on hand, and feeling sorry for Marty, they agreed to use him as an official roadie. Marty was a self-proclaimed guitar aficionado, and he had an ego like no other. He also thought he was God's gift to the ladies of the world. He was also a tad bit on the lazy side. Needless to say, it took very little time for everyone in the band and crew to develop a deep disdain for him. The manager tried to talk to him about the issues, to no avail. In his defense, he was somewhat trapped, all tangled up in those family ties, so he really couldn't fire Marty mid-tour, no matter how bad he was. The rest of the band was not happy about keeping him around, but they were stuck with him as well. It seemed the more they tried to ignore Marty, the more obnoxious he became. With all the spare time they had traveling from town to town and hanging around backstage before shows, the annoyance of Marty was amplified, till it simply became too much to bear.

I'm not sure which of the guys came up with the idea, but it was probably the bass player, because it was as brilliant as it was devious. Not only that, but the execution was flawless. In today's world, one just cannot function without being involved in some type of social media. Of course there is Facebook, which everyone uses, but there are also many other sites based on specific interests. There are hunting groups, political groups, religious groups, and dating sites out the wazoo. It just so happened that one of these social media outlets was the perfect weapon for getting back at Marty.

I had never heard of a site called Grindr, but apparently, it is something like Facebook, specifically for gays. A check-in function allows members to post where they are, a function often used to arrange on-the-fly hookups. I have a sneaking suspicion that you already have an idea where this story is going, but we'll continue.

One night when the bothersome Marty was not around, the guys got together and created a Grindr account for him. The profile made him appear incredible, larger than life, and they used his real name and photo. From that day forward, every place they went, in every bar or club they played in, someone checked Marty in. Of course he had no idea what they had done, so he could not figure out why gay men kept coming on to him at bars, clubs, restaurants, laundry mats, and even at Walmart. Since he was as heterosexual as one could be, to the point of being a bit homophobic, it was a devastating blow, so to speak, to his ego.

I cannot believe the band has been able to keep quiet about it, especially when they witness the attempted hookups. I think the plan is to delete the account after this road trip, since they informed the manager that Marty would not be heading out with them in the future, under any circumstances, but I would not be surprised if they accidentally on purpose forget to delete it.

What's the very important moral of this story? One should never be a jerk in the presence of bored musicians. Otherwise, it will bite you in the backside.

Hey, Man, We're with the Band

Yes, music, babes, beer, babes, gigs, and babes all go together. Did I mention the babes? Even if they won't admit it, many-a-guy has gotten into music simply because of the chick factor, and just as many have had to leave music for the same reason. Of all the songs that have been written throughout all of time, the vast majority are about or to a woman, subtracting all the Elton John ones we now know were not. Lovely ladies inspire us to write, encourage us when we are down, allow us to buy equipment when we can't afford it, put up with us staying out all night, learn to live with our basement practices, and, more often than not, pay the bills, since most musicians don't really make any money. Often, they smack us in the head with that great big two-by-four called reality: "Honey, we have six kids and live in my mom's basement, so you need to get a real job." Suffice it to say that babes are not only very important to the music business; they are a must, absolutely critical. Now, before the femi-Nazi element starts screaming at me, I will admit that there are many wonderful female musicians out there who work just as hard as male ones do, but this is my story, and I'll write what I want, so please just take a great big dose of shut-the-hell up! Also, the fact remains that far more men are out gigging every weekend, statistically speaking, so this chapter in particular is much more relevant to the boys in the band.

I need to make a clear distinction between wives, girlfriends, babes, and groupies in reference to musicians. Wives usually do not attend every gig, as they are the ones who have to work real jobs to pay for your hobby career. Even though they are supportive, they are also probably your most reliable critics. If your wife says, "Give up the black leather pants and play less Iron Maiden," you had better listen to her.

Girlfriends usually accompany you to every gig, even when there's not enough room in the van; they have no trouble squeezing onto your lap. They always tell you how great your performance was, even if your guitar was out of tune, the PA distorted the vocals, and the drummer started everything way too fast, then sped up some more. Unlike wives, a girlfriend can and usually will create friction between you and the rest of the band, and this friction will more than likely lead to a band breakup.

Babes, on the other hand, are what musicians live for, at least the unattached musicians. These are the hot-looking, young, scantily dressed women who show up at gigs and often become the better half of a one-night stand. A good example is the subject of Lynyrd Skynyrd's "What's Your Name?"

Finally, there is the groupie, a strange sort of woman, possibly deranged. Her one goal in life is to be with a member of the band. They are almost always too old or too young and not nearly attractive enough to be called babes. Some just bed down with musicians as notches on their belts, for bragging rights. They are usually permanent fixtures of the club and hit on all the musicians who pass through, so they are not all that dangerous. On the other hand, some groupies are more like stalkers and will follow a particular band or musician from gig to gig. Avoid the *Fatal Attraction*-type groupies at all costs, or you might just see your bunny boiled in more ways than one.

I have had my own experiences with babes, girlfriends, and even groupies, but I also want to add that for the past thirty-five years, I have had the great privilege of being married to one of the most supportive wives a musician could have. That said, I could probably write another twenty stories about the bodacious vixens I encountered in my career as a musician. Instead, though, I will focus on several girlfriend stories.

First up is my very first band girlfriend, someone who completely defied all the above rules for a band girlfriend. Of course she thought it was cool to have a boyfriend who was the lead singer in a popular rock band, but only as long as it didn't interfere with my time with her. We had so many fights because she begged me to come over but I just couldn't because my band needed me for a jam session. During our last argument, she shouted, "You just watch! I'm gonna get between you and that band of yours." I sure do miss her.

Throughout my bar band days, girlfriends came and went, as they usually do in that particular lifestyle. Now that I think of it, in their defense, it must be very hard for chicks to put up with the over-inflated egos most musicians have. After I left the bars and got involved in the Christian rock scene, it seemed I would settle down and treat women better. After all, aren't Christians supposed to operate by the Golden Rule, treating others the way they want to be treated? Truthfully, and much to my chagrin now, I was much worse then than I was during my bar days. I found myself often dating several women at the same time. What was worse, without even realizing it, I made them all feel as if they were the only one. In hindsight, I probably knew they felt that way, but I was way too chicken to deal with the truth, so I just let them believe we were exclusive, in an effort to spare them from hurt. That dishonesty burned me a couple times. The first time it bit me in the butt was when I was dating a girl we will call Mindy.

Mindy was a nice, really good-looking girl, and we dated for a long while, but to be honest, I just didn't have strong feelings for her. Thus, while we were dating, I looked up an old girlfriend from my bar days and invited her to some yet-to-be-determined gig. I mentioned her before, the Wisconsin chick, the cousin of my former lead guitarist. In passing, I mentioned to my friend Rudy that I was playing a gig at a coffeehouse, and I invited him. I didn't actually expect him to show up, but I thought it would be nice to ask him anyway. On the night of the gig, I took Mindy, my actual current girlfriend, with me. As fate would have it, Rudy decided to bring his cousin with him, the Wisconsin chick. My only salvation that night was the layout of the coffeehouse. It was an L-shaped design, with the stage at the junction of both legs. Mindy sat on one side, and the Wisconsin chick was on the other, so they could not see each other. I ran back and forth between the two all night, wearing myself out entirely, physically and mentally. When I finally caught Rudy alone, I asked, "Why did you bring her with you?" He replied, "Well, she said you invited her," to which I desperately shouted, "I didn't think she would come!" I told Rudy I was there with another woman and convinced him to take the Wisconsin chick home, but man, I was almost toast!

Did I learn my lesson that night? No way! In fact, just a few weeks later, my band played at an all-day music festival with several other bands, and of course Mindy went with me. Earlier that week, I met a sweet young girl named Tori, and I told her about the festival and even stupidly said, "It'd be great if you can come." Of course it wasn't a date, because I already planned to take Mindy; I only invited Tori to be kind and let her know I was available for a possible future date, when Mindy wasn't with me. Tori was no dummy, so I'm sure she knew exactly what I was up to, even though she didn't know Mindy or that I was dating her. At the festival, Tori sat directly behind Mindy and listened as she told a friend all about the future she expected to have with me. Mindy informed her friend that she was going to leave for Florida for several weeks and that she very much expected a wedding proposal upon her

return. All the while, the eavesdropping Tori wondered why I had invited her

to the festival, but she didn't say anything to Mindy about it.

With Mindy off in Florida, it was the perfect chance for me to ask

Tori out on an actual date. Rather than just one, we went out every night for

two straight weeks. By the time Mindy returned from the Sunshine State, that

wedding proposal had already been made, but it wasn't offered to her. Mindy

didn't have a clue about Tori and me, and she actually found out via a phone

call from a friend while she was still in Florida. I'm quite sure she was very

pissed, though I never really knew for sure, because I didn't have the nerve to

face her. It's been thirty-six years now, and I'm still married to Tori and

haven't spoken a word to Mindy since. I'm such a coward!

Why Didn't You Tell Me I'm Black?

Denver is one of the funniest men on the planet, and when he tells this story, people hold their sides in pain from the laughter. I'm sure I can't do it justice, but it has to be told all the same. Before jumping into it, though, let me tell you about the comedian himself.

Denver is a tall, lean, very good-looking, talented, black man who has spent most of his life around white people. He attended a primarily white university on a music scholarship, and most of his gigs are with white bands. He is also married to a beautiful white woman. Thus, it's safe to say he is comfortable in the company of Caucasians, even when he is the only black man in the room. I spent a couple years in a band with Denver, and we had a lot of fun playing the whole black/white thing. On one road gig, we had to pick him up in front of his day job in downtown Cincinnati. Five white guys in an unmarked van pulled up in front of a crowd, with Denver standing in the middle. We slammed on the brakes, threw our side door open, and two of us jumped out, grabbed Denver, and threw him into the van, then took off.

The looks on the faces of that crowd were priceless, and I was surprised they didn't call the cops!

I don't care how integrated or how unprejudiced we say we are. The truth is that many Caucasians have difficulty with their own feelings in the company of blacks. This doesn't apply to everyone, but it does happen for a great number of white people. Denver is a mastermind at picking up on this uneasiness, and he loves to play with people because of it. Once, Denver and another black musician/vocalist played a gig at a Christmas party in a very ritzy revolving restaurant high above Covington, Kentucky, overlooking the Cincinnati skyline. The event was attended by a bunch of old, rich folks, very stiff and very old money. There wasn't a black man in sight, other than Denver and his music partner. The gig went well, but as they were packing up to go, an old guy in a wheelchair stopped Denver. "That was real nice," he said. "We need more of your kind in here."

Denver knew what the guy meant but decided to toy with him a bit. "Our kind, huh?" he asked with a feigned scowl. "You mean…musicians."

"No, no," the man said. "I mean…your kind."

"You mean young guys, right?"

"No! You know what I mean! *Your* kind."

"Yeah, yeah, I get it," Denver replied. "You're talking about vocalists."

"No," the man said, beginning to get irritated.

The banter went on for several minutes, until the guy finally got pissed and rolled away, without once mentioning to Denver what he really meant.

Man, I Feel a Lotta Love Here Tonight

After my nightclub days were over, I joined a Christian rock band. I have already written about the changes in my life that led me to that, so I won't rehash that here. Suffice it to say that it was huge change. One difference was the quality of music. In the bars, I played cover music, but in the Christian band, all our tunes were originals. The musicians were also a lot better. The only problem was finding gigs. It was the mid-seventies, at the forefront of Christian rock as a genre, and there just weren't many bands like us around. Bars didn't want us to play our Jesus music, and churches didn't want us because our music was supposedly of the devil. Man, talk about being between rock 'n' roll and a hard place! We had no choice but to be trailblazers back then, and I'm sure today's Christian musicians have no idea what we went through to open the doors for them. Now, there are venues galore, but back in those days, it was tough.

Let me tell you a bit about Bema, some real rockers. We probably could have been classed as hard rock, with just a touch of jazz. Each member of the band wrote music, bringing our individual taste to it, but once a tune was brought to the group, all our individual styles fused within the song to give it an extremely original sound. At the time, there was nothing like us in the Christian music world. There were a few bands around, but very few offered the quality of music and musicianship of Bema.

Once, during the pursuit of gigs, we contacted a local rock station that was sponsoring a summer festival, in the hopes of landing a spot onstage. As it turned out, we were a few weeks late in contacting them, and all the spots were filled by the time we called, but they did inform us about another opportunity. A women's prison had contacted them to ask if they were aware of any bands who would be willing to travel to their location and give a concert. Man, we were all over that, and what a perfect fit it was. We were a band with a message, and they definitely needed to hear it—not to mention that they would, quite literally, be a captive audience.

Another thing about Bema was that we were never preachy, even though we were a Christian band. We did have a message, as I mentioned, but our lyrics said it all for us. The fact is that if listeners didn't pay careful attention to the words, they might not have even recognized that we were a Christian band. We were not ashamed of being Christian, but we didn't flaunt our faith either. We considered ourselves a rock 'n' roll band that just happened to sing about something a whole lot more important than getting laid. That leaving-it-to-the-lyrics idea was also very unusual for Christian bands of the day, and it was a point of contention between us and others in our genre. Most threw their beliefs in the faces of others. I already told you the story of one such band, along with several of their so-called disciples, stopping by one of our practices to drop off several religious tracts about the occult. Instead of being upset, we actually got a huge charge out of that and even joked about renaming ourselves The Camp Springs Occult Blues Band.

Anyway, we made contact with the prison and scheduled a concert date. Needless to say, they did not know we were a Christian band, and many didn't realize it even after we performed. We drove for several hours to get to Belleview Bottoms, Kentucky, out in the middle of nowhere. The directions they gave us were: "When you think you've gone too far, go another twenty miles," and I'm not making that up!

When we finally arrived, we set up outside. After our sound check, they let the women out in the yard. I can honestly and unequivocally say I now know exactly what a nicely built, mini-skirted woman walking past a construction site feels like. The growls, the wolf whistles, the cheers, and the shouts indicating just exactly what they wanted to do to and/or with us were absolutely outrageous. Those inmates knew exactly what went where and why, and they wanted to make sure we had not forgotten ourselves. I've played in biker bars, whorehouses, and every other kind of hole-in-the-wall imaginable, but I had never felt so embarrassed in my life.

We finished the set, and our new girlfriends shuffled back inside in their very unflattering, state-issued jumpsuits. We made the long journey home, wondering if some of the things the girls mentioned were even

physically possible.

Closing

I'd Do It All Over Again, but This Time, I'd Want More Money!

Was It Worth it? What Did I Learn?

Well, we've finally come to the end of this book. Quite possibly, somewhere in the pages preceding this one, I've pissed off what few friends I had left. Believe me, that was not my goal. You are all valuable contributors to the local music scene, and your stories simply have to be told. I did my best to protect your identities, but if anyone thinks they recognize you and asks if a particular character is you, simply follow the guidelines of your modern-day politicians: Smile, lie, and deny. On the other side of the coin, many of you whom I have jammed with may wonder why you weren't included. To you, I say, keep a lookout for the sequel, because I'm sure you'll find yourself somewhere in those pages.

Was it worth it, my journey as a musician? Absolutely! I love being a musician. Just being onstage, in front of a crowd, giving my all and watching the audience respond is worth every trial and heartache that comes along with it. Better still are the people I've met and had the honor of sharing the stage

with, an honor undeserved. Thank you for that!

Sure, I'd do it again, but there are some things I would change. I'm

definitely not proud of everything I've done, especially the drugs and alcohol.

I'm certainly not proud of the way I treated some folks along the way. Hey,

I'm a musician, so I'm not all that smart and was bound to screw up. Overall,

the experiences of being in a band and playing on the road have made me

who I am and enabled and equipped me to deal with life.

What did I learn? Well, that could very well be another book in itself,

but I will briefly mention a few things that come to mind. First, know your

skill level and play what you can, with all the intensity you can muster. I once

heard Abraham Laboriel, one of the world's best bass players, say, "If all you

can play is the root note, then play it with all your heart. If you can run the

fret board, great, but play it with all your heart." What a wise man! Set realistic

expectations but try to beat them. If you set your goals too low, you will not

improve, but if you set them to high, you will set yourself up for

disappointment. Remember, few are called, and even fewer make it.

I've heard it said that Chet Atkins was asked if he could read music.

His answer was, "Not enough to hurt my pickin." With all respect to one of

the greatest guitar players ever to bless this planet, I must humbly disagree. I

play by ear and have often found it to be a great disadvantage. For sure, you must be able to play by ear as well as improvise, but reading music, as well as understanding music theory, can open worlds of opportunity.

Do not trust managers and club owners, because they will screw you over. Church musicians, don't blindly trust what an event organizer tells you. They are not necessarily trying to do you wrong, but they often find themselves in over their heads and may steer you wrong.

Treat your bandmates right. You are no better and no worse than they are, even if you have different skill sets and levels of experience and knowledge. Remember that if you screw over a bandmate, sooner or later, word will get around.

Finally, don't ever give up, no matter what. Situations may change, and you may not have as much free time as you used to have, but I encourage you to find a way to keep playing, even if it's just a half-hour after everyone has gone to bed. Perhaps you now have some physical complications to contend with. If you do, find a way to play around them. The Def Leppard drummer lost an arm but set up electronic triggers to compensate, using his feet. I lost part of my left index finger but learned to play with the other three and finally switched over to bass. If you are truly a musician, you simply must play. When you are not playing, not only will you get rusty, but you will also lose precious time when you could be learning and improving. I foolishly dropped out and did not touch an instrument for a few years, and that is one of the biggest regrets of my life. Don't do that to yourself, not for any reason whatsoever.

Most of all, brothers and sisters in the band, keep the faith!

Where Are They Now?

I've maintained close ties with many of the folks I've jammed with, but several have moved on, and I have no idea where they are or what they're up to now. Some have even left this Earth, but I like to believe they are now happily jamming with Jimi, Janis, and Otis. Here, I'll provide a few quick updates about some of the musicians you've read about in these stories.

Charlie

Charlie knocked up a friend of my wife's and denied the child. I haven't seen him in about thirty years. I heard he got married and still lives in our hometown, and I recently received a message from him via one of his friends through Classmates.com. He left a phone number, but he did not return my call. I also found out he's still drumming in a country band.

Sam

Sam passed away unexpectedly. The band kept playing, but we chose not to have a front man in the future, as a way to honor him. Instead, we took turns introducing tunes, and I gave the vocalists cues from behind my bass, so they knew when to start. Sam, we miss you, and I know you now have a voice that can keep up with Aretha's. In a few years, when the rest of us join you, let's get the band back together.

Denver

Denver is still active in church music. He and his wife have two of the most beautiful kids I've ever seen. I haven't seen him in about seven or eight years, but my son ran into him at a music conference a few months ago and told me that Denver is still as crazy as ever.

Jack Snow

Jack remains one of my best friends, and we talk on the phone from time to time. He still plays on occasion, albeit nothing very serious. The rest of the time, he keeps busy running his business.

Andy

I talk to Andy quite frequently. He has not played in several years and has actually given away all his equipment. Since he is very close to retirement, I suspect and hope he'll pick up his instrument and start playing again.

Jake

Jake passed away many years ago. He farmed and fiddled up to the day he died. I want to do the same, jam right up to the moment I see St. Peter, and then the gig will really kick in!

Rudy Taylor

Rudy was my very best friend and the greatest influence on my musical interests. He passed away unexpectedly a few months ago. I had not talked to him in several years and did not know about his passing until two months later, when his wife found my business card and called me to tell me. Rudy, I love ya, man! In large part, I am who I am because of you.

Jamie

After several stays in the local jail, Jamie headed for the West Coast and really whacked out. He now looks like a reject from a Grateful Dead concert and earns his living making drug paraphernalia that he claims is only for novelty use.

Rocco

Rocco still plays. He lives near Cleveland and works for a microphone manufacturer. He is married, with four kids, two of them adopted from China. He spends every lucid moment of his life trying to make his way to Tennessee.

Matthias

Matthias is the real success story among the characters I've written about. He continues to write and play gigs. He is a full-time music director at a large church and is also studying for the ministry.

Wally Spicer

Wally married and divorced, then took off to follow some religious icon out West. Some touring musician friends of mine ran into him several years ago in New Mexico, where he was supposedly working on nuclear bombs for the government. I believe he is now in Tennessee.

Luke Schneider

Luke is a story all his own. He headed to a small town in the great Southwest. It was rumored that he threw a dart at a map and headed wherever it ended up. For a while, he traveled up and down the West Coast, playing music. I found him on the internet, and we traded a couple email messages. As far as I know, he is now herding goats on some undisclosed mountaintop.

Ronnie

Ronnie's current whereabouts are unknown to me. About thirty-five years ago, he headed off to work on the Alaskan oil pipeline, but I have heard nothing since.

Jonas

I saw Jonas at a club not long ago. He seems to perpetually seek the Fountain of Youth. The last time I saw him, he had his very thin hair permed and dyed jet black. He still dresses like a 1970s lounge lizard, but he also still plays, and that's the most important thing.

Tim

Tim was not mentioned by name, but he does appear in several stories. He is a now minister. He is still writing and jamming and has turned out a couple nice CD projects. He and I do some distance recording projects via email; I send him a scratch track, and he sends back the guitar track. Isn't technology great?

Jerry

Jerry is married and is also a youth pastor at a small church. He also plays in a classic rock band with a bunch of old fogies.

Pete

Pete will never stop playing, and I just know he'll take his drums with him to the old folks' home someday. He's currently in three bands, and he has the most supportive wife a musician could have. Bud, keep living the dream!

Freddie

Freddie is still singing off key in the same music group. I don't think anyone has ever found enough nerve to tell him to give it up. I've not talked to any of the guys in that group for years, but I bet they are still muting his microphone during each performance.

Mr. Woods

Mr. Woods was promoted to assistant director in charge of pencil sharpening or some other similar job, just to get him away from the day-to-day management of the school. He has long since retired, and I have no idea what he's doing, but he could quite possibly be the hall monitor at an old folks' home somewhere in Florida.

Jason

Jason's current whereabouts are unknown, although he did become a wedding singer after he left the band. I wanted to use him in my wedding, but my bride-to-be refused, since there were too many musicians on the guest list already. For all I know, *The Wedding Singer* was really about him. If it was,

Adam Sandler did a pretty good job.

The Wisconsin Chick

At this time, her whereabouts are unknown, but she may very well be

in Wisconsin.

Scott

Scott is another guy who took off to in pursuit of a religious icon. I

heard he is married to a really nice woman who keeps pays all the bills, since

he is not too interested in work.

Mick

The last I heard, Mick was working as a sales rep, but I believe he is

also still jamming.

Chip

I see Chip quite frequently, and I'm confident he will never stop

playing, although these days, he does way more recording than playing. In

fact, he has become a fine recording engineer in his own right, and I

understand that his eighties band is getting ready to do a reunion tour.

Terry Adams

Terry's whereabouts are currently unknown, but I hope he either gave up playing or took lessons.

Denny Horgan's Traveling Revival and Show

Denny is still plugging away as a traveling evangelist and singer. His kids are all grown and no longer take part in the show, so it's just him and his wife. He's starting to age now, so I'm not sure if he can still make that jump from the stage to the front pew.

Markie

Markie's whereabouts are unknown.

The Fools

All the guys from the band are still out jamming, albeit not with each other. They get better and better every day. Keep the faith, brothers!

Troy

Troy left the church band and went into the studio to record his original music that was rejected by the band. He now opens for several professional Christian bands with his own group of musicians, and he makes sure to accept input from each and every member of the band.

Jonathan

Jonathan went into full-time ministry as an evangelist. As his kids grew, he taught them to play various instruments, so they now have a family band, and nowadays, he's just about the happiest person I've ever met.

Lynn

It's such a shame, but Lynn no longer plays. Maybe his excuse is that he sprained an ankle running around the building. He is still involved, though, because the company he owns manufactures drumheads. I'm sure he's making more money doing that than he would drumming for a living, so maybe that worked out for the best.

Wayward Son

The members of the band ultimately went in several different directions. While it's hearsay at best, it's assumed that one guy is a minister, one is a carpenter, and one is in computers. I do know one still plays, because I caught several of his performances not long ago.

Marty

The manager's cousin eventually broke up with Marty, so no one felt obligated to invite him back on the road with the band. He did discover the Gindr account, but he had no idea who opened it. A potential hookup asked why he bothered to post on Gindr if wasn't interested in a date, and he was beyond pissed.

The Almost Ready for Divine Time Players

These guys are still chugging along and will sing anywhere, anytime, at a moment's notice. They dropped—or, should I say, lost—the band and now sing along with an accompaniment track. This probably works out better for them, since they can literally stand on any street corner and vocalize with a boom box for backup.

The End